with best wishes
to
Desmond.

Taxicabs

A photographic history

by

Philip Warren

and

Malcolm Linskey

ALMARK

Almark Publishing Co. Ltd., London

First Published 1976.

ISBN 0 85524 268 X

Printed in Great Britain by
Chapel River Press,
Andover, Hants,
for the publishers, Almark Publishing Co. Ltd,
49 Malden Way, New Malden,
Surrey KT3 6EA, England.

CONTENTS

ACKNOWLEDGMENTS

The Authors make grateful acknowledgment to the help given to them by the following: P. B. Kavanagh, Assistant Commissioner of Police (Traffic); R. S. Ainsworth, J. Everitt and J. Orr, Public Carriage Office; R. Overton, Mann & Overton Ltd.; G. de Ciantis, London General Cab Co.; Alan Withey; Maxwell Green; Frederick Crowton; Louis Baum and Roy Cummins, Royal British Legion Knowledge School; Miss Plank, Commissioner's Library; Mr Robinson, Science Library Annexe; Staff of the Guildhall Library; British Leyland; Vauxhall Motors; Ford Motor Co.; F.I.A.T. Motor Co. and Renault Motor Co. The Authors would also like to express their particular appreciation to Mrs Patricia Linskey for her invaluable assistance in producing the typescript.

The Authors are grateful for permission to reproduce photographs which appear on the following pages: National Motor Museum 12, 17, 19, 20, 27, 29, 34, 40; Vauxhall Motors 14; London Transport 15, 42, 54, 55; Renault 21; Alan Withey 25, 28, 30, 31, 38, 41, 45, 46, 47, 48, 49, 50, 51, 52, 53, 67, 68, 69, 70, 71, 72, 73, 74, 75, 76; Greater London Council 43, 61; Fiat 50; London General Cab Co. 56, 91; London Fire Brigade 59, 60, 62, 94; British Leyland 64; Derek Pearce 79; Mann & Overton Ltd 80; Max Green 80, 82, 87, 89; W. H. Cook & Sons Ltd 81; Terry Higgins 82; Carbodies Ltd 84; British Resin Products 88; Taxinews 90; Lucas Industries 92. All other illustrations belong to the Authors' private collections.

Cab ranks c. 1650 This view of Westminster by Hollar shows lines of horse-drawn cabs waiting outside Westminster Hall. In the centre one has just set off with a fare.

Introduction

In these days of mass production and standardisation, the purpose-built Austin FX4 London type taxicab is to some extent remarkable. Often called 'old fashioned' because of its appearance, it nevertheless embodies all that is best in public passenger vehicles. Almost three centuries of 'Conditions of Fitness' dictated by Parliament have combined to produce the world's finest taxi. The 'Conditions of Fitness' for motor cabs were first laid down in 1906 and have since been modified as occasion demands.

The story of London's cab trade really begins in 1654, when Oliver Cromwell authorised the setting up of the Fellowship of Master Hackney Coachmen. Control lay with the Aldermen who were also responsible for making the necessary byelaws in the City of London. Unfortunately, religious and political differences eventually forced Cromwell to disband the Fellowship in 1657.

In 1662, Charles II's 'Cavalier' Parliament passed an act for the improvement of roads, by-ways and sewers; the money for these improvements was to come from the licensing of London's hackney coachmen who were to pay £5 per annum for their licences. The Act was to run for a term of 17 years, but when it terminated in 1679 there was no Parliament in session to pass another act. Thus it was not until 1688 that the coachmen were again licensed. Their status was regularised in 1694 (5th & 6th Will. & Mary Cap. 22) and since then control has always been by Parliament.

The 1694 Act constituted the Hackney Coach Office and five Hackney commissioners who were directly answerable to the Treasury lords. Under Cromwell 250 coaches had been licensed to ply for hire but as London grew so did the number of coaches and by 1831 they numbered 1,200. The 'interests of the public' have always been the prime consideration of the licensing authority. For instance, the 1662 Act laid down the minimum size of a horse needed to pull the heavy and cumbersome coaches, 'no horse or gelding or mare to be used with such coaches shall be under the size of 14 hands high'.

In 1679, what is believed to be the first provisions for the safety of land passenger vehicles were made when the Commissioners laid down 'Conditions of Fitness' for hackney coaches: 'the perch of every coach shall be 10 feet long at least and have cross leather braces before and not braced down, but hang upon a level, not higher behind than before, and the coach shall be strong and large enough to carry four persons at least'. (Almost 150 years previously an act of 1555 had prescribed safety regulations for boats that plied for hire on the Thames.) Both new and second-hand hackney coaches were also required to conform to these specifications. Therefore the cast-offs from the nobility that came to do service as hackney coaches had to be modified. In many cases, however, the insignia of the former

Public Carriage Office c. 1884 The Hansom and Growler featured here are outside the Metropolitan Police Public Carriage Office awaiting inspection. The Public Carriage Office was located at Scotland Yard, Whitehall, and it was this association with the Metropolitan Police that led to the famous Norman Shaw building being erected on the site at a later date.

owners were not erased from the doors.

The London Hackney Carriage Act of 1831 (1st & 2nd Will.IV Cap. 22) repealed all former legislation relating to London's hackney carriages (as distinct from stage coaches) though some clauses from the previous acts were included in the new legislation. The Hackney Coach Office was abolished and the licensing powers were transferred to the Commissioner for Stamps. At the same time all limitation on the number of hackney carriages were removed. In 1838 (1st & 2nd Vict. Cap. 79) the drivers as well as the owners were licensed, and the Commissioner of Stamps was replaced by the Registrar of Public Carriages. (In 1850 this office was abolished.) The act of 1843 (6th & 7th Vict. Cap. 86) gave authority to the Commissioner of Police for licensing owners and drivers. For the first time a driver was required to wear a metal badge with his licence number printed on it. On vehicles however it had been necessary to paint the licence number on both doors of coaches, between 1654 and 1714. Since then, a metal plate fixed to the back of the cab has shown the vehicle licence number.

The act of 1853 (16th & 17th Vict. Cap. 33) consolidated the acts of 1843 and 1850 giving complete control of the London cab trade to the Commissioner of Police, causing a furore of protest at the time from the trade and from the press. 'No one person should have such absolute power' said the *Sunday Times*. 'The responsibility of the police is towards persons and property and not to run hackney carriages' said trade representatives.

Perhaps Parliament was of the same mind for in 1869 (32nd & 33rd Vict. Cap. 115) control was vested in the Home Secretary who in turn was to delegate his authority to the Commissioner of Police. The licensing of vehicles, owners and drivers was to be carried out by the Public Carriage Office, via the Assistant Commissioner of Police (Traffic). This is still the current arrangement. For some years the staff of the Public Carriage Office have been civilian, although at Scotland Yard there is still a Cab Enforcement Section whose duties cover offences committed by cabmen and anyone else in breach of the Hackney Carriage laws.

In the past many people criticised the stringent conditions laid down by London's cab licensing authority and though perhaps there was room for genuine criticism it is only because of the Public Carriage Office, backed up by the Commissioner of Police, that London today has the finest cab service in the world. Any such criticism for the last 100 years should be directed at Parliament for various Home Secretaries have overridden proposed changes. The 'Conditions of Fitness' are examined from time to time by the authority of Parliament and alterations are based on the Home Secretary's authority. If changes are desired then the Public Carriage Office will implement them, for they are there to administer the law but do not change it.

The first coaches which were actually designed for hire work did not appear on the London streets until 1823. These were the 12 cabriolets belonging to David Davies of Mount Street, Mayfair, using a rank in Great Portland Street, near to Oxford Circus. They were two wheeled, lighter and were a distinct improvement on their cumbersome predecessors; their shape quickly earned them the nickname of 'Coffin cab'. In a short while the yellow and black painted cabs became extremely popular, partly because they charged only two thirds the price of an ordinary fare.

> In days of old, when folks got tired,
> A hackney coach or a chariot was hired;
> But now along the street they roll ye,
> In a shay, with a cover, called a cabriolet.

The last of the old hackney coaches was taken off the street in 1848, probably much to the satisfaction of Charles Dickens, who had written, some time earlier,

> A hackney coach – fogh! who can be a gentleman and ride in a hackney coach, who can indeed, to predicate nothing of stinking wet straw and broken windows and cushions on which the last dandy has cleaned his shoes and of the last fever it has taken to Guys and of the last load of convicts it has taken to the hulks.

With the ending of the limitation on the number of hackney carriages in the 1831 Act, the streets of London were open to everyone. Previously the short stage coaches could only operate on a fixed route beyond the area of the Bills of Mortality, defined as that area where returns of the deaths in the parishes were drawn up as a 'Bill' and accounted for, since 1603, by the Worshipful Company of Parish Clerks. In 1831 the area of the Bills extended roughly from Whitechapel in the east, to Marble Arch in the west and parts of Islington and Hackney in the north to Southwark in the south. Within this area 1,200 hackney coaches had previously been licensed to ply for hire, whereas the short stage and long stage coaches could only pick up at a central point, but were not allowed to set down until they had travelled beyond the area of the Bills.

The short stages, now able to pick up and set down along their entire route, rapidly passed through this transitional stage, gradually formed into major bus companies, and eventually were organised as London Transport. Notable among these companies were Thomas Tilling, who ran both cabs and buses, and Goode & Cooper Ltd of Brixton, who also ran cabs and buses during the nineteenth century, but who, with the coming of the motor bus, went over to motor cabs and only ceased trading in the 1970s.

The Act of 1831 had terminated an era of 177 years during which London's licensed hackney carriages were the only form of public transport except for sedan chairs, within the capital. Apart from the river service provided by the watermen, who themselves were replaced by hackney coaches, these hackney carriages performed exactly the same function that taxis do today.

The removal of limitation in 1831 encouraged competition and thus had a marked effect on vehicle development. Edward Boulnois introduced a new cab in 1832. It was two wheeled and closed in; the driver sat on top, in front. As the door of this cab was mounted at the rear, it was easy for passengers to alight before the journey's end, without paying. This gave it the nickname of the 'Bilkers Cab' and it was short lived.

In December 1834 Joseph Aloysious Hansom registered his Patent Safety Cab. The main principle of Hansom's design was the cranked axle and the body hung low to the ground, but the driver as with the Boulnois cab sat in front. Hansom sold his rights in the cab for £10,000, but it is believed he never received the money. By a strange quirk of fate Hansom's name has been a synonym for a cab that was not really his at all. In 1836 the Secretary of the Two Wheeled Cabriolet and Two Wheeled Carriage Co. was John Chapman. He recognised the defects in Hansom's cab and invented improvements which changed the basic design, placing the driver's seat in its now familiar place at the rear; the sliding window was introduced, and the framework under the body was constructed to rest on the ground when tilted backwards or forwards.

The company that owned Hansom's cab quickly purchased Chapman's Patent and, within a few months, some 50 of these cabs were working on the streets of London. They were such a success that other proprietors wanted them and soon imitations, almost identical to the real ones, began to appear. The Hansom Cab Co. was determined to protect its rights, and legal proceedings were taken and in every case they were successful. But frequently the losers were men of straw and the company could not recover its damages. They were compelled to stop litigation and the pirate owners were given a free hand.

Few people could tell the difference between a real Hansom or Chapman and its many imitations, though the drivers could, and they treated the pirates with contempt. They called them 'Shofuls', a slang word of Jewish terminology meaning counterfeit. Many Jewish drivers worked for the original company and they conferred this term on all vehicles which infringed Hansom's and Chapman's Patents. The word 'Shoful' eventually became a slang word for Hansom cab.

When the Hansom Cab Co. took over Chapman's Patent they still continued with the words 'Hansom's Patent Safety Cab', so that the public could recognise that the cab belonged to the same firm as the cab that Hansom had patented. Therefore, Hansom's fame should rightfully be Chapman's.

At the same time as Chapman's cab appeared in the streets there was another type of carriage introduced, built by the same David

Hansom cab 1836
The Hansom, originally introduced in 1834, was modified in 1836 by John Chapman. Improvements in design continued throughout the nineteenth century. The last licensed Hansom was withdrawn from London service in 1947.

Clarence (Growler) 1837 Designed by David Davies in 1836, and modified to this design in 1837, this cab remained virtually unchanged until the last Growler retired from service in 1948. These particular Growlers belonged to the famous cab and bus operator, Thomas Tilling.

Davies who had introduced the cabriolet in 1823. It was constructed to carry two passengers inside a completely enclosed compartment and one passenger next to the driver on a seat that projected out from the body of the main carriage. It was first known as the covered cab. Within a year David Davies made improvements so four passengers could sit inside. This was the vehicle which was to become known officially as the Clarence and colloquially as the 'Growler'. Whether it gained this nickname because of the noise its wheels made on the cobbled streets or because of the temperament of its driver is a matter for conjecture.

One other Hansom type cab was to make its appearance; this was the tri-bus. This cab, designed by Mr Harvey of Westminster Bridge Road in South London, was licensed in 1844. It had several refinements, including the driver's seat being offset, so that he could open the passenger door, which as with the 'Bilkers Cab' was at the rear. It was capable of carrying three passengers and it had two small wheels fitted at the front to prevent it pitching forward if the horse stumbled or fell.

With the exception of Harvey's tri-bus and the experimental quarterbus, which was the invention of a Mr Oakey, the Hansom cab and the Clarence were to reign supreme until the early years of the twentieth century, when they were ousted by the internal combustion engine.

On 2 July 1868 the Society of Arts had decided to award its Gold and Silver Medals for various types of hackney carriages for two persons, open and enclosed, and the best hackney carriage for four persons, either open or enclosed or both. The response was not very fruitful and the offer was dropped. However, in 1872 they revived the idea, after the cab proprietors had said that they were reluctant to incur expense unless cash prizes were offered. The Society withdrew its Medals award and substituted cash prizes. These were £60 for the best improved cab of any description, £20 for the next best two and £10 for the following two. The conditions were that the cabs must be ready for the Exhibition at South Kensington in 1873 and that the judges must be satisfied that the cabs had been working on the streets of London for three months. The judges were the Duke of Beaufort, Lord Arthur Somerset, Major General Earley-Wilmott, Lord Alfred Churchill and Colonel Henderson, Commissioner of Police. To give the judges some professional status they also included a coachbuilder, a cab proprietor and a cab driver, the last three being unnamed.

Sixteen different vehicles were entered, but the judges could not find one that was an outright winner. However, they decided that four of them were worthy of sharing the prize money equally between them. They were C. Thorn of Norwich; Mr Lambert of 66 Great Queen Street, Holborn; Forder & Co. of Wolverhampton; and Messrs Quick and Mornington of 8 Netherwood Street, Kilburn. The following Saturday these four cabs were lined up at Marlborough House for an inspection by His Royal Highness, the Prince of Wales. He was so impressed with Forder's cab that he ordered one from the company for his own use.

The most important of Forder's improvements was the reintroduction of the straight axle. This was achieved by cutting away the body of the cab under the passenger seat. He also raised the driver's seat some 7 feet above the ground. Thus he achieved the perfect fulcrum. The driver's weight counterbalanced by the shafts meant a perfectly balanced vehicle. In addition as the weight was taken off the horse it was possible to maintain a high speed and greater manoeuvrability.

Some 20 years later the Society prided itself that the Hansom cab designed by Messrs Forder of Wolverhampton had been extensively adopted in London, and that any improvements made during those 20 years could be attributed to the offer of prize money by the Society.

Flushed with the success of the first Exhibition, the Royal Society decided to hold a special Exhibition, this time at Alexandra Palace. A prize of £200 was offered for the best cab and cab driver with the longest employment with one employer, who had never been charged with cruelty to his horse, been drunk, insolent or guilty of reckless driving – an impossible task if the columns of *Punch* are to be believed.

The Exhibition was held on 4 October 1875 and Forders won the prize outright, displaying once again the firm hold they had on the design and manufacture of these 'Gondolas of London' that were now capable of obtaining a speed of 15 to 17 m.p.h. But not all the credit can go to Forders. Between 1843 when Mr Harvey had patented the seat attachment for Hansom cabs to 1868 when Mr G. Clark invented the folding hood, no less than ten other men had patented improvements incorporated in the final version of the Hansom of 1875.

As late as 1894 Mr Thrupp of Maida Vale, London, offered prizes for the best cabs on four wheels, probably as an attempt to do for the Growler that which the Society of Arts had done for the Hansom. The cabs were to carry two or more passengers with luggage, the hood was required to fold and the driver had to sit in front. Keynotes were durability, simplicity and accuracy of construction. Thirty designs were received and they were exhibited at the Carriage Bazaar in Baker Street.

It was too late, the age of the motor vehicle was upon them, Karl Benz's first production car had been on the roads since 1893, and the writing was on the wall for horse-drawn cabs. By 1905 Hansoms and Growlers were diminishing at the rate of 600 a year. The refusal of London's cab drivers to accept the taximeter until it was forced on them by legislation in 1907 was the main reason for the late introduction of the motor cab. However, by 1908 the transition was such that a linkman's one blast on the whistle for a Hansom cab was now used to call a motor cab, the Hansom had become second best.

Bersey (Humming Bird) 1897 Operated by the London Electric Cab Co. Ltd, this was the first mechanical taxi in Britain. The vehicle was similar to a Clarence four wheeler carriage. The bodies were built by the Great Horseless Carriage Co. and later models by the Gloucester Railway Wagon Co. The electric motor, with its pronounced 'hum', was a 3½ h.p. Lundell type. The power was supplied by 40 batteries of 80 volts each, giving a maximum speed of 9 m.p.h. and a range between charging of 30 miles.

Prunel 1903 London's first petrol cab. Put into service by the Express Motor Service Co. with Hansom style bodies by the famous carriage builder, Henry Witlock & Co. of Holland Gate, London. There was a drop-seat alongside the driver for an extra passenger. It was supplied with a two cylinder 12 h.p. Aster engine which developed a maximum speed of 25 m.p.h.

Transition

'For years to come you have little to fear from the invention of the motor car, but in ten years, perhaps, electric cabs would [sic] be in use.' So spoke Sir George Sitwell at a dinner given by Scarborough cabmen in February 1897. Just six months later, on 20 August, 14 electric Bersey cabs left the depot of the London Electric Cab Co. in Juxon Street, Lambeth.

Designed and constructed by C. W. Bersey, the 'Humming Birds', as they were called, were capable of attaining a speed of 9 m.p.h. and a range of 30 miles. The body weight of 14 cwt combined with the accumulator gave an overall weight of 28 cwt. Like David Davies' cabriolets of 1823, the Bersey cabs were also painted yellow and black, giving them a distinctive appearance. When these cabs first appeared on the streets, the other cabmen were dumbstruck. The London Cab Trade Council condemned the enterprise and protested against the further licensing of such vehicles.

The Metropolitan Police Commissioner in his Report for 1897 said, 'The 18 hackney carriages propelled by electricity appear to have given general satisfaction, the vehicles are roomy, the interior well fitted and the mechanism is well under the control of the driver. Should electric carriages come generally into use, the effect upon the traffic of the Metropolis will be marked, as such vehicles occupy little over half the space of that of a similar vehicle drawn by a horse'.

In the spring of 1898 the original cabs, then numbering 24, were withdrawn and were replaced by an up-dated version. In order to reduce vibration, the body was now slung on an entirely separate set of springs from that which the motor and accumulators were supported. The accumulators were larger, enabling the maximum speed to be increased from 9 to 12 m.p.h.

The new cabs were much noisier than the earlier models and breakdowns became so common that drivers began to fight shy of these cabs. An incident outside 38 Hyde Park Gate caused a mild sensation when a cab ran out of control, causing considerable damage. The adverse publicity this received, plus the fact that they were proving more expensive to run than had originally been anticipated, forced the company to take them out of service, in 1899.

There was then a temporary respite for the horse-drawn cabs until 1903, when the first petrol driven cab, the Prunel, was licensed. The first Prunel ran unchallenged for nine months; then in 1904 two more were licensed. Very little is known about this French built cab and by the end of 1904 they had disappeared from the London cab scene.

Many drivers have, at one time or another, claimed to be the first motor cab driver, but this distinction definitely belongs to James Howe, who, in August 1933, was presented

Left **Rationals 1905** Produced by the Heatly-Gresham Engineering Co. Ltd of Letchworth, these vehicles were run by the London Motor Cab Co. Ltd of Manor Street, Chelsea, in red livery. The bodies were built by Messrs Saunders of Hitchin, Messrs Wilson of Royston, and Messrs Maythorn of Biggleswade. The engine was a two cylinder horizontal, 10-12 h.p. with a two speed epicycle gear change. All were withdrawn in 1909.

Far left **Vauxhall 1905** This was Vauxhall Motors' only venture into the cab trade, and this model was put into service by the Metropolitan Motor Cab & Carriage Co. of Sussex Place, South Kensington. The engine was a three cylinder, 7-9 h.p. with a three speed gearbox and was chain driven. By March 1906 all five that had been in service had been withdrawn.

Right **Herald 1906** Although still Hansom in pattern, these cabs were introduced as the successor to the Vauxhall by the Metropolitan Motor Cab & Carriage Co. Ltd. The fleet of 15 was London's largest in 1906. Withdrawn by 1907 because passengers had difficulties alighting from them past the driver's seat. The engine was a two cylinder of 10-12 h.p. and was French built.

Ford 1906 This was the only Ford taxicab to have been licensed in London, although Ford did build a provincial taxicab in 1932. The only three supplied were operated by the Automobile Cab Co. of Chester Gate, Regents Park. The Automobile Cab Co. had to place in the side lamps a green glass with a large white 'A' in the centre, in order to identify the company's cab to prospective passengers. The engine was a four cylinder, 20 h.p. one supplied on a model B chassis with epicycle gears.

with a special badge by Lord Trenchard, then Commissioner of Police, at a ceremony held at Scotland Yard. Mr Howe, then aged 75, lived in Wellesley Avenue, Hammersmith and had held a licence for 49 years. He sold his horses and cabs in 1894 and when the first Prunel came along he was chosen by the Express Motor Service Co. to drive it. The badge now hangs, with others, in a special collection at the Public Carriage Office.

The Vauxhall Co. was the first well-known name to become associated with the London cab trade and in 1905 built five cabs for the Metropolitan Motor Cab and Carriage Co. The Vauxhalls were highly regarded by the drivers, as the cab possessed all the features of the old Hansom, which made it easily recognisable as a vehicle plying for hire. This was an important feature as the public was unaccustomed to hailing motor cabs, and it also influenced the motor cab companies in their choice of the early vehicles. The Automobile Cab Co. of Chester Gate, Regents Park, withdrew the Vauxhall motor Hansoms from service within a year because passengers found the lack of visible control unnerving.

The Rational cab, licensed in 1905, more closely resembled private cars of the period. Only 11 of these cabs were licensed and they were painted in the red livery of the London Motor Cab Co. Ltd, whose premises were at 93 Chelsea Manor Street. The water cooling system was of the thermosyphon type with two sets of radiators; solid tyres were fitted to all four wheels. The bodies were built by various companies and it was the first London motor cab to give complete all round protection from the weather for the passengers.

In 1906, the Metropolitan Cab Co.'s Vauxhalls were replaced by Heralds, which still continued the Hansom design. This was a two seater cab with central drive. The driver's seat was movable to allow for easy passenger access. Because of the difficulty of identification, these early cabs tended to work from ranks. It also appears that they were designated certain ranks by the management, who advertised on tariff cards, 'Herald cabs can be obtained by telephone from the garage, the Hyde Park Corner rank or the rank at Trafalgar Square at any time'.

In March 1905 the 20 h.p. model 'B' Ford with a top speed of 40 m.p.h. had been exhibited at the Agricultural Hall in Islington. The Ford agent in England was the Central Motor Car Co. Ltd of 117 Long Acre. The car sold for £175 and to stimulate public interest in the vehicle, Mr Perry, the managing director, arranged for conversion of the three landaulettes to cabs. To comply with Police Regulations they had to be capable of turning round in 25 feet. They were also painted white to make them recognisable to the public. The cabs were licensed in 1906 and were driven without much difficulty by three ex-horse cab drivers: Messrs Crow, Chambers and Clarke.

Argyll 1906 This formidable machine was Argyll Motors' first attempt to enter the cab trade. Typical of early motor cab prototypes, it proved unpopular because of the difficulty of accessability to the engine for routine maintenance. The engine was a powerful 16 h.p.

Right **Unic Brasier 1906** This model built on a Georges-Richard chassis was introduced by Mann & Overton Ltd. It was popular with fleet operators and with owner drivers who thought it looked extremely smart. It was supplied with a two cylinder 10-12 h.p. engine.

Below **Unic Brasier 1908** This four cylinder version of 12-14 h.p. was introduced for town and provincial private hire clientele. It had a well finished four seater body by Christopher Dodson Ltd.

They were the only Ford motor cabs to be licensed in London. Two hundred had originally been ordered but only five seem to have been delivered to the Automobile Cab Co. because Fords were not satisfied that the firm was commercially sound. They were correct in this assumption because by 1910 it was out of business. It also had more than its fair share of 'rip off merchants' who in the absence of taximeters were inclined to charge a customer according to his appearance.

With the refusal of Fords to supply more cabs, the Automobile Cab Co. turned to another quarter, namely, France. They ordered 40 Sorexes, a 14 h.p. cab especially designed for work in London. On Saturday 27 October 1906 this company lined up 30 Sorex cabs on Victoria Embankment between Charing Cross and Waterloo Bridge. S. Michaels manager of the firm said, 'In order that the public can distinguish the company's cabs from private cars we are staging this exhibition; we shall also be placing a letter A on the glass of the side lamps.'

Horse-drawn cabs had never had any form of identification, and it was not until 1910 that roof signs appeared on London's motor cabs, the first one being fitted to a Panhard in April 1910. The roof signs proved extremely satisfactory and other models soon adopted them, and they have remained a prominent feature on cabs ever since.

Between 1903 and early 1907, many different makes of vehicle were tried on the London streets. Generally, only one or two were licensed; many were not. Some of the names of these early cabs are familiar, but others, like shooting stars, were seen for a few moments of glory, then gone. Such vehicles were the Adler, Mascot, and Adams Hewitt – though this latter was to reappear a few years later as the plain Adams cab. The Simplex, Sorex, Jeantaud, Renault and Unic were all jostling for a place in the London cab scene, where the Renault and Unic were soon to become famous. The embryo motor manufacturers were quick to realise that if they could produce a successful London cab their reputation would be considerably enhanced and the public would be encouraged to purchase one of their cars – a point quickly appreciated by the Ford agent in London.

The Carl Opperman Electric Hansom Cab, imported from America, was displayed at the Town Carriage Competition held at York

Left **Marples 1907** Built by Stephen A. Marples of High Holborn as a replacement for the horse-drawn Broughams of the London Improved Cab Co. The two cylinder vertical engine had mechanically operated valves, developing 12 h.p.

Below **Pullcar 1907** This unusual front wheel drive cab was manufactured by the Pullcar Motor Co. of Preston. The large Hansom cab type wheels at the rear reputedly gave a smoother ride. Even for 1907 this vehicle was considered outdated and few, if any, were licensed, despite a remarkable turning circle of less than 20 feet. Both two and four seaters were produced. Each had a four cylinder engine, developing 14-16 h.p.

Road, Waterloo, on Monday 14 October 1906. It had a wheel base of 6 feet 6 inches and a track of 4 feet 7 inches. The framework of the chassis was of pressed steel; the overall length was 10 feet and it weighed 29 cwt. However it was never licensed for London, though it was fitted with a taximeter.

Another exhibit was a Unic motor cab, manufactured by Richard-Brasier of Paris. It swept the board in the Competition taking a first for body work; first for stopping and gear changing without jerks or noise; first for comfort of passengers and easy access; and first for smoothness of running. It was second in its class for ease of manoeuvrability, and fourth for the ease of cleaning the bodywork and machinery, including oiling.

This was a tremendous achievement, fully justifying its name of Unic (unique). Thus began a quarter of a century's connection

A neat and effective combination.

Turns in a circle of less than 20 feet in diameter, without reversing: see, also, photo on next page.

with the London cab trade. Originally operated by the City & Suburban Motor Cab Co. Ltd, of Avonmore Road, Kensington, the Unic was soon taken up by other companies and by 1914 it had become a market leader. World War I interrupted the import of this cab from France, but by 1920 the production line was flowing again and continued to do so until 1928. An attempt was made between 1928 and 1930 to build a British version, but the cost proved to be prohibitive. Until 1928 the cabs were distributed by Mann & Overton Ltd.

Mann & Overton were founded in 1899 by J.T. Overton, father of the present managing director, Robert Overton. His partner was J.J. Mann, who lived in Paris. It was from this connection that the firm obtained the sole agency to distribute Mercedes-Benz cars in England until 1905, when this was relinquished and the agency for the Unic taxi was started. J. J. Mann retired in 1907, and J. T. Overton was joined by his brother, William. A surprising number of Unics were sold in the years prior to World War I and J. T. Overton would visit Paris once a month to ensure that production was proceeding to the Public Carriage Office requirements; often he would drive a Unic back to London.

Dawfield, Phillips (D.P) 1907 This cab was renowned for its simple design. It had a twin cylinder horizontal engine mounted half way between front and rear axles, driving a single chain. The turning circle was a remarkable 20 feet.

In the first motor car race to be held in England at Bexhill on Whit Monday, 19 May 1902, J. T. Overton won a fine silver cup, and shortly afterwards was the first man to drive non-stop for 1,000 miles under the close scrutiny of the R.A.C. From 1905 Mann & Overton specialised in taxicabs in premises in Ebury Bridge Road, near Victoria station. They had another showroom in Lower Grosvenor Place for the sale of cars. Both premises were given up after World War I and the company moved to Battersea Bridge Road; they bought their existing property at 296/8 Wandsworth Bridge Road in 1938.

Despite the success of the landaulette motor cab, there were still people who insisted on continuing with a horse cab body design. As late as 1907 the Pullcar Motor Co. of Preston, Lancs., was still trying to promote a front wheel drive cab with large 'Hansom' type rear wheels. Both two and four seater versions of this motorised horse carriage were produced. Although the Pullcar cab was built as a direct competitor to the Growler and met the requirements of Scotland Yard, few if any were licensed in London. Heavy luggage work at railway stations was possibly the only field in which the horse-drawn Growler was still holding its own.

But at least one of the large and old established horse cab companies was aware that this situation could not last. The London Improved Cab Co. Ltd, then London's largest horse cab company, with over 500 cabs and 2,000 horses, employed Stephen A. Marples of High Holborn to build a motor cab capable of seating four passengers with proper provision

for the volume of luggage encountered at stations. The resulting design was strongly influenced by that of the Growlers, as the roof was made strong enough to take luggage. The design was particularly favoured by the drivers because of the ease in handling luggage up onto the roof rack.

The early problems of transition were about to be resolved by a 'bombshell' which burst on the London cab scene in March 1907 – the 'Renault' cab. Its introduction greatly influenced not only the cab trade but the board rooms of major motor manufacturers in England, France and Italy. The largest single order at that time then placed for a motor vehicle anywhere in the world had been announced; the Renaults were about to make their presence felt.

Renault 1906 This cab's dramatic introduction created a French dominance of the London cab trade.

Pre-war boom

The arrival of 500 Renault taxis at the General Motor Cab Co.'s garage on the corner of Camberwell Road and Brixton Road early in 1907 caused a sensation. On 21 March the company invited the Press to a preview of the garage, although the cabs had in fact commenced work two days previously. After lunch, the members of the Press were escorted round the garage, which had space for 1,000 cabs.

The two seater Renault cabs were virtually of the same design as the cabs then working in Paris, and were fitted with a two cylinder, 8-9 h.p. engine and a three speed gearbox. Since June 1906 the company had been operating one of the French built Renaults, fitted with a taximeter. This was the first known instance of one being used on a London taxicab, although there had been previous attempts to fit them on horse-drawn cabs. Although taximeters were not made compulsory until later in 1907, the General Cab Co. Ltd were adamant that they were not running cabs without them, and they had been steadily recruiting drivers pledged to take out cabs with the 'jewish pianos' or 'zeigers', as they called them.

The company itself was severely criticised for going 'foreign', because not only were the vehicles French, but a good deal of the capital also came from France, mainly from the Compagnie Generale des Voitures. The General Cab Co. Ltd merged with the United Cab Co. in 1908 to form the London General Cab Co. though both were to continue running as separate companies. As late as 1934 the 'London General' still had its 'French connection' via the Banque d'Alsace et de Lorraine and the Compagnie Generale d'Exploitation, though both companies were by then in the hands of the Paris Receiver.

Considerable controversy surrounded the Renault cab. On 4 January 1911 J. S. Pritchley, a member of the R.A.C. Club, read his paper entitled 'The Evolution of the Taxicab' to members of the Club. During the discussion that followed, H. Sturmey told the audience that the 'Conditions of Fitness' drawn up by Scotland Yard in 1906 requiring a 25 feet turning circle and 32 inches between the outside edge of the front springs were impracticable, and the Society of Motor Manufacturers and Traders had objected to them. This new regulation was intended to give the cab greater stability for the safety of the public yet at the same time to enable the vehicle to turn round in one movement. The engine had to be mounted some way back, and several companies were experiencing great difficulty with this part of the regulation.

By the time British companies including Humber, Argyll and Adams had overcome this problem, the French Renaults were on the streets. Meanwhicle Mr Sturmey had discovered that the distance between the front springs of one Renault was 26 inches instead of 32 inches; this made a whole difference to

Adams (Pedals-to-Push) 1908 Produced by the Adams Manufacturing Co. of Bedford. Supplied with either a two or four cylinder engine with a friction band clutch; the epicycle gears of three forward speeds and a reverse were all individually pedal operated, hence the sales line 'just pedals-to-push', which led to its nickname.

Argyll (Mustard Pot) 1908 A cab of more conventional design by Argyll Motors. A prominent feature was the engine, gearbox, clutch, countershaft brake and striking gear, all being combined as a removable single unit. This was the first cab successfully to incorporate 'cricket seats'. The colourful Argyll livery was responsible for the descriptive nickname. The engine was a four cylinder, 12-14 h.p.

Right **Humber De Luxe 1908** This four seater cab was produced as a De Luxe version for prestige town work. Unfortunately, like the early Argyll, the lack of accessability to the engine was its downfall. The four cylinder engine was housed on a wheel base nearly 2 feet shorter than the standard type. Priced at £350, it was only £25 dearer than the alternative model.

Below **Humber chassis 1908** A view of the two seater cab chassis introduced by Humber in 1908, clearly showing the four cylinder, 10-12 h.p. engine.

the design of the cab. He wrote to Scotland Yard pointing out that the Renaults which had been licensed did not come up to the official requirements. Scotland Yard replied that it was true, those vehicles did differ, but they were experimental and it was thought that in the interest of the public they should be given a trial.

Clearly, the regulations had been relaxed to suit the French company, at the expense of their British rivals. The 'Conditions of Fitness' were subsequently altered in 1907 and British built cabs followed within the next two or three years. However the Renault was the forerunner of many more types of cab.

Humber 1908 This cab, the standard version by Humber Motors of Coventry, proved a great success. Built with the same four cylinder engine but on a longer wheel base than the De Luxe model, it was in 1908 the cheapest cab on the market. It proved very popular with mushes, although Humber Ltd operated their own fleet.

Scotland produced the Argyll which, when it appeared in 1906, was a very cumbersome vehicle that does not seem to have been licensed in London. It was succeeded by the 12-14 h.p. four cylinder engine version early in 1908 and some 40 of these saw service by 30 September of that year. A striking feature of this cab was the combination of engine, clutch and gearbox in one self-contained unit, which could be removed with the minimum of trouble. The gearbox was three speed and reverse and the changes of gear were effected through a gate by a hand lever.

This vehicle also boasted another innovation. It was the first cab to have 'cricket' seats, where two extra passengers could sit with 'their backs to the 'orse'. Unfortunately, the engine proved uneconomical, and as it was the driver who paid for the fuel there was considerable reluctance on his part to take them out. However this cab found favour in America, and 50 Argylls were exported there and run by the Universal Taximeter Cab Co. of 153/157 East 53rd Street, New York, who

Darracq 1908 A popular French built cab first used in London by the giant General Motor Cab Co. A two cylinder and a four cylinder engine was available. An unusual feature of this cab was the gearbox, which was, to some extent, combined with the differential gear and back axle. An added touch of luxury were foot warmers for the passengers.

Darracq 1908 This cab was basically the same as its predecessor, although the gear driven water pump was abolished and the radiator was put across the front of the dashboard. This re-styling of the bonnet meant that the cab now looked almost identical to the Renault. As well as being used in London and Paris, 300 cabs of this model were supplied to New York.

Thames 1908 In an attempt to diversify this cab was built by the Thames Ironworks, Shipbuilding & Engineering Co. of Greenwich. A noticeable feature was the wormdriven back axle powered by a two cylinder 12 h.p. engine with a metal cone clutch. The first models were operated by the Motor Cab Syndicate of Cannon Street.

hired them out to the Knickerbocker Hotel on Broadway. They were imported in chassis form by John H. Naughton, who had spent some weeks in England looking for suitable vehicles. On arrival in the U.S.A. the chassis were sent to Boston for the construction of the body.

Humber Motors of Coventry built two versions of their cab, though only the standard type saw service in London. Because it was the cheapest cab on the London market it became very popular with mushes. It also provided plenty of luggage space on the roof, unlike many of the smaller two seater cabs. By the end of September 1908 some 84 were licensed; 47 were owned by the Humber Cab Co. Ltd of 32 Holborn Viaduct and the remaining 37 were owner driven. One of the first three mushes in London was W. W. Withey of 65 Ethelred Street, Kennington, who purchased the first Humber cab to be licensed in 1908. His son, C. J. Withey of Thornton Heath, Surrey, followed his father into the trade, but he has now retired. W. W. Withey's grandson, Alan Withey, is probably one of the finest restorers of vintage cabs in Britain today.

However the French dominance still persisted, this time with the Darracq, produced as a two cylinder and four cylinder cab. There were 333 Darracqs licensed by September 1908: 229 were owned by the United Cab Co., a subsidiary of the 'London General'; nine by another 'General' garage of Old Jewry; the Stanhope Motor Cab Co. of Gloucester Gate, Regents Park owned one; and the remaining 94 were owned by the London General Cab

Co. itself. Their fleet now consisted of 643 Renaults, 37 Wolseley-Siddeleys and the 94 Darracqs, a total of 774 cabs, making it most probably the largest fleet owner in the world. By this time the New York Taxi Co. were also using 300 Darracqs.

'Mush' or 'mushing', denoting an owner driver, is said to have derived from this early Gallic influence. It was used in the same context as the French Canadian fur trapper calling to his dog team, 'mush, mush', meaning always on the go, or keep going. There were probably other French sayings used in the early days of motor cabs, but only the word 'mush' appears to have survived.

By Act of Parliament in 1907 all cabs were required to have a taximeter fitted, and, though there is insufficient space to go into the complexities of the meter problem, we must make some mention of it. In the absence

of an adequate distance and time measuring device, altercations between passenger and drivers were common, women being particularly vulnerable. Nearly every writer on the subject from De Saussure, in the eighteenth century, to *The Times* of the twentieth, had always made out the driver to be the villain of the piece, and there is little doubt that many were. However, not all drivers overcharged; for instance, James Quaife, in the foreword of his book on hackney coach charges published in 1825, said 'To the drivers who frequently charge less rather than more than they should'.

To find a device that would accurately measure time and distance had baffled many people, from the ancient Chinese to British, French and German inventors of the late nineteenth century; the credit finally went to Herr Bruhns of Madgeburg in Germany, about 1890. In 1910 the Bruhns Taxameter Co., which was operating from 245 Gray's Inn Road, introduced a new meter with drum counters, instead of discs, and the meter showed 'Stopped' on the dial. At the outbreak of World War I this company changed its name to the British Taximeter Co., and was eventually absorbed into the Kienzle Co. of

Far left **Belsize 1908** Against the heavy French competition, this cab produced by Belsize Motors of Manchester was sold as the 'all-British cab'. Either because of reliability or patriotism, this cab soon established itself as a leading make. It was available as a two seater with a four cylinder 14-16 h.p. engine with a metal cone clutch. Note the three-quarter landaulette style – rare at this period.

Left **Greenwood & Batley (Electromobile) 1908** Built for the Electric Taxicab Co. to compete with Growlers for heavy luggage work at railway stations. Powered by a 45 cell battery with a single motor of 8 h.p. The total weight of the cab was 30 cwt, which allowed for a stout body and heavy batteries.

Fiat (Type 1) 1908 A popular Italian cab used in Rome, Paris, New York and London. The Fiat Motor Cab Co. operated its own flee in London of over 400 cabs, all with a four cylinder, 12-15 h.p. engine with a multiple disc clutch. The fuel consumptior of 28 m.p.g. was a redeeming feature. For the passengers a special attraction was an indicator giving instructions to the driver of 'left', 'right', 'faster', 'slower' and 'home'.

West Germany, who market the 'Argo' meter in Britain via Lucas Services (U.K.) Ltd. In an attempt to stem the flood of motor cabs, owners fitted meters to their Hansoms and Growlers.

Undoubtedly, the most successful meter, in terms of numbers, is that produced in Sweden by Haldex and marketed in Britain by Halda Ltd of Brandon Road,·York Way, London. The first Haldas were designed in 1898 and, although the Halda Co. was not formally constituted in this country until 1911, their méters were fitted on London motor cabs in 1907. The London company received many letters from people in countries where Halda meters were used including the Chief of Police in Warsaw, Moscow Weights & Measures Department, Fiats of Bologna (Italy) and the British Motor Cab Co., who, in 1910, changed over to Halda meters for their entire fleet of 1,000 cabs. In 1910 the seven meter companies made an agreement only to supply meters on a hiring basis, an agreement they apparently hastened to ignore.

Between the wars, the parent company in Sweden was often in dire financial trouble and was only kept going by money received from England. In the 1929 Depression the situation

Wolseley-Siddeley 1908 Built by the Wolseley Tool & Motor Car Co. and available with a two or four cylinder engine which was capable of being set to run at a pre-determined minimum speed by means of a lever on the dashboard. The two cylinder engine was of 8-10 h.p. and the four cylinder of 10-12 h.p. This cab heralded a long association with the trade by Wolseley-Siddeley.

Wolseley-Siddeley chassis 1908 A side view of the two cylinder, 10-12 h.p. engine mounted on the distinctively shaped Wolseley-Siddeley chassis.

Lotis 1908 With a compact two cylinder V-type engine and 'foolproof' two speed epicycle gearbox, this cab was probably the shortest ever built, but had an unusually large luggage space.

became worse when the annual rental charge per meter dropped from £7.50 to £4.25 per annum, and it seemed unlikely that the company could survive. By 1937 the number of Halda meters had fallen to 900, but this proved to be the nadir of the company's fortunes. A few months later they introduced their Mk 5 model and by the outbreak of war in 1939 almost 1,000 had been installed, and demand was increasing.

Of the seven meter companies who signed the agreement in 1910 only two (Halda Ltd and the British Taximeter Co.) remained in the early 1950s. Two new companies entered the market but, by 1975, they had gone: Metropolitan Fare Registering Co. just ceased to exist and Bell Punch was acquired by Halda in 1975. The British Taximeter Co. was taken over by its German supplier. The introduction of the electric model Mk 8 in 1960 gave Halda a really competitive meter and, once more, Halda reclaimed the dominant position it had held some 50 years earlier. By 1976 the number of Mk 8 meters has increased to more than 22,000, and the majority are rented.

To describe fully every type of taxicab built between 1903 and 1976 would require the scope of an encyclopaedia. Some, however, are of particular importance. The Rover, Austin and Wolseley-Siddeley are all famous

Lotis chassis 1908 This side elevation of the remarkably compact Lotis chassis highlights the space saved by the two cylinder V-shaped engine.

names in the motoring world, but the fine reputation of these companies rests four square on the cabs they introduced to London and the experience they gained by doing so.

The first Rover cab was exhibited in London in July 1907 and the first cab was licensed later that year, several hundred Rovers eventually seeing service. As with the Argyll, the two cylinder engine was mounted as one unit with the clutch and gearbox. The front spring was of the transverse type and even at this early date Rover had gained a reputation for comfort. Previously the company had only produced the one cylinder and four cylinder type of chassis, but for economical working in London the two cylinder version was considered more suitable.

The Austin Motor Co. were working on a cab in 1906, but were experiencing difficulties with the Public Carriage Office regulation concerning the 25 feet turning circle. The cab

Star (Sunstar) 1908
This popular two seater landaulette cab was built by the Star Engineering Co. of Wolverhampton, which was famous at the time for its touring cars. The cab prototype was a four cylinder, but a two cylinder, 9 h.p. version proved more acceptable. A foot pedal operated the powerful metal-to-metal hand brake on the gear shaft. This cab was popular with jobmasters for day hire.

Below **Charron (C.G.V.) 1908**
Already established as bus builders, Charron Motors introduced this cab to gain a share of the booming British taxi market. The cab had a two cylinder 8-10 h.p. engine; the clutch was a very broad faced cone, giving three forward speeds. Final drive was by a propellor shaft to a live rear axle. This type of vehicle was added to the French dominated fleet of the General Motor Cab Co.

De Dion-Bouton 1908 Yet another French built cab of fine repute. This particular vehicle was famous for the ease of accessability to all working parts, particularly the two cylinder, 10 h.p. engine. An interesting feature was the unique dual system of high tension magneto and coil ignition. De Dion-Bouton at a later date introduced a single cylinder version.

Rover 1908 Built by the famous Rover Co. of Coventry, this cab incorporated a specially designed two cylinder engine which, together with the clutch and gear casings, was bolted together to form one unit. The suspension in the front was a single transverse spring designed to absorb road indentations.

they exhibited at the Motor Show held at Olympia in 1907 showed that they had resolved this problem by mounting the engine underneath the driver. The engine, clutch and gearbox were all mounted on a subsidiary frame which was itself suspended at three points through rubber buffers; thus the engine was completely insulated from road shock. This arrangement was completely original and it produced excellent results, for it enabled the maximum lock to be obtained without loss of track. The driver sat in the centre with luggage space available on either side. The bonnet was snub nosed, and the whole cab was very compact. British Leyland apprentices have, in recent years, restored one of these cabs and it is now kept at Longbridge near Birmingham. The full story of the Austin cab comes in a later chapter.

The Wolseley-Siddeley cab was notable for the comfort given by its three-quarter elliptic springs. It lasted about six years in London service, but by 1911 it was already being phased out. The reason for this is obscure, but it is known that many drivers had difficulty handling the cab. A Public Carriage Report in January 1912 stated 'that the Siddeleys wanted humouring'. Probably they were withdrawn from service because they were only two seaters, and the drivers who had won the right to the Extras on the meter in 1911 simply would not drive them. Some 450 of these cabs

Napier 1909 Built by the Napier Cab Co. of Acton Vale, London, it was available with either a two cylinder, 10 h.p. or a four cylinder, 15 h.p. engine. Both models were supplied with a metal-to-metal cone clutch and a three speed gearbox combined as one unit. The main operator of this cab in London was the famous W. & G. du Cross Co. This vehicle was one of the first British cabs to have been exported, particularly to the Commonwealth.

Brouhot 1909 French built, this particular cab was a four cylinder, 12-14 h.p. version, although a single cylinder cab was also available. The final drive was through a propellor shaft and bevel gearing to the live back axle. This cab, like the Fiat, included an electric communicator for directing the driver to turn 'left' or 'right' etc.

were produced between 1908 and 1912. The London United Motor Co.'s fleet numbered 250, and 100 were owned by the London & Provincial Cab Co.

From the middle of the nineteenth century, drivers were required to be tested on every type of cab they drove. From a licence issued in 1909 to Percy Brown of Leander Road, Brixton, we find he could drive a Panhard, Napier, Fiat, Vinot, Gladiator, Unic (Gate) and Unit (Quadrant). Many drivers failed the driving test for second and third types of cabs, as the gears, clutch and brake pedal and accelerator varied from model to model. For example, the Charron and Siddeley had side notched change speed quadrants; the Renaults were bottom notched; and the Unics top notched. The Charron differed from the Siddeley in that the hand brake was applied by pushing; in the latter the brake was pulled. The Renault had a brake and clutch pedal combined – a feature no other cab had, at least prior to 1912. The speed of the Siddeley cab was controlled by both hand and foot, whereas the Renault and Charron had provision for hand setting on the dash, with foot control as well; the Unic had foot control only.

On average between 1908 to 1912, one fifth of all drivers failed the first test and a quarter of those failed the second test, though very few failed the third time. Superintendent Bassom of the Public Carriage Office reported to the Assistant Commissioner of Traffic in 1912 that 'One fifth of the men who wanted to drive other types of cabs would have been incompetent had the present testing system not prevailed. I submit that the figures given prove beyond a shadow of a doubt that no change is possible in the present system.'

In 1908 the Public Carriage Office issued a regulation that passengers could not sit next to the driver. On some cabs this was not possible, as only the driver's seat was fitted; however, several makes including the Humber, Rover, Marples, Argyll, Unic, Renault and the Fords did have a seat for a passenger next to the driver. This second seat was removed on all existing models and phased out in new ones, and so it has remained to this day. The immediate advantage was, of course, somewhere to put the luggage. The Lotis cab manufactured by Sturmey Motors Ltd of Widderington Road, Coventry, was the first cab built with a specially designed luggage platform next to the driver, with 9¼ square feet of luggage space. Until this space was created and luggage racks were fitted, the old Growlers had managed to hold their own against the motor cab.

In 1903 there had been 7,499 licensed Hansoms, 3,905 Growlers and one motor cab. Within ten years the Hansoms were down to 386, and the Growlers to 1,547, but the number of motor cabs had increased to a mammoth 8,397. The Hansoms had decreased at a rate of up to 1,000 per year and they were being sold off for firewood at £1 each. Even after luggage space was provided on motor cabs the Growler was still supreme in the stations, because the railway companies would not allow motor cabs on to their premises, because of insurance problems. This was resolved in 1910 and almost immediately the Growler was doomed. Between 1910 and 1914 they had declined from 2,721 to 1,159.

Frequently there was no protection from the elements for the driver or luggage though some cabs did have canopies over the driver. Other makers experimented with windscreens but in May 1910 the Commissioner of Police expressly forbade any glass screen in front of the driver, 'in the public interest'. It was not until 1934 that a full screen was allowed, provided there was fitted a device to wipe the screen when it rained.

In 1908 the greatest number of different types of cabs were produced. One of these the Electromobile was powered by battery and built by Greenwood & Batley of Leeds for the Electric Taxi Cab Co. Ltd of 7 Hertford Street, Mayfair. Only 20 of these were licensed and they were intended mainly to cope with the heavy luggage involved in station work. It was soon withdrawn because it had a range of only 45 miles, 10 miles less than the average mileage per shift. The Star cab was another short lived cab, although it subsequently had some success as a Jobmaster's vehicle, i.e. private hire car.

The most successful British cab of the period was most probably the Napier, built at the Napier works at Acton, mainly for W. & G. du Cross Cab Co. also of Acton. It was extremely successful both in London, the provinces and in parts of the Commonwealth where it was exported in large numbers. Altogether some 900 were licensed for London; 700 two cylinder, 10 h.p. cabs, and 200 of the four cylinder, 15 h.p. version.

The Fiat, built by the F.I.A.T. Motor Co. of Bologna, Italy, was also notable. Some 2,100 Fiat cabs were produced of the 1908 version and saw service in London, Paris and New York. It had a top speed of 44 m.p.h. at 28 m.p.g. The cab could accommodate four passengers plus the driver and was capable of carrying 330 lb of luggage. Apart from alterations in body design, the engine and chassis were largely unchanged for ten years. It was operated in London by the F.I.A.T. Motor Cab Co. Ltd of 153 Luper Street, Pimlico. In 1908 they took delivery of 37 cabs, and eventually their fleet numbered 400; by then their main garage was in St Pancras Road, King's Cross.

Vinot 1909 This French cab was remarkable in that it was introduced to Britain by Messrs Oates Brothers, a suburban motor cab service in Wimbledon. The reliability of the four cylinder, 14-16 h.p. engine used in their service led to a wider distribution in Britain.

This great profusion of cabs did not last. The boom of 1907 was finally exhausted, and, for many, the end was bitter. By 1910, several large companies, including the Reliance Cab Co., Express Motor Cab Co. and the Consolidated Cab Co., had been wound up. Something was wrong. When the London General's balance sheet of 1910 was published there was a credit of £1,700, a sharp drop from the previous year's £83,000.

Many motor cab companies that started in 1907 and 1908 after the 'London General' 'bombshell' did so in complete ignorance of the trade and inevitably many costly mistakes

Gamage-Bell (Birdcage) 1910 This cab company, formed by the famous Holborn Emporium and Horace Bell, ex-manager of the General Motor Cab Co., specialised in building its own bodies on various chassis. The cab shown here is based on a four cylinder, 15 h.p. Napier chassis, fitted with the unique Gamage-Bell standard limousine body with the unusual door opening angle. The large side windows with the wired glass explains the nickname.

Gamage-Bell 1911 This photograph shows the only known open carriage type body ever fitted to a cab. Introduced by the Gamage-Bell Motor Cab Co., it was built on a Napier chassis. Licensed by the Public Carriage Office in London to carry two passengers.

were made. They were just entrepreneurs. On the other hand by 1910 67 per cent of all motor cab drivers were ex horse cab drivers and they knew what 'the game' was all about. When the Home Secretary laid down the fare scale in 1907 it was set at 8*d*. per mile and 2*d*. every quarter of a mile. It was purely experimental. No one had ever run motor cabs before, at least not on any large scale. The motor cab companies had no idea of what the depreciation would be, nor how cabs would work in traffic. Most important of all, they could not possibly foresee that they would have to pay part of the fuel costs, and that the drivers would retain the Extras; both of these commitments increased the proprietors' operating costs.

When the fare had been agreed in 1907 the question of the extra charge for more that two passengers, and luggage, had not been resolved. Since the 1853 Act, the Home Office had determined the scale of Extras to be charged, but who had them was a matter between owners and drivers. Until 1907 the horse cab drivers had always kept the Extras, simply because there had never been the means to record them. The installation of taximeters changed this. The 1907 Act clearly stated that all the fare must be shown on the meter, including Extras. The proprietors then claimed that the Extras were theirs to offset running costs. This dispute lasted from 1907 to 1911 when a Government Committee of Enquiry awarded the Extras to the drivers. This the companies claimed cost them £45,000 a year.

The early motor cabs were mainly two seater and two cylinder. They were

Hurmid 1910 Little is known of this two cylinder, 12 h.p. cab other than it was operated by Messrs Hurst & Middleton of Holloway.

Napier 1910 This impressive line up features the standard four cylinder, 15 h.p. Napier and is part of the 1,000 cab fleet of W. & G. du Cross of Acton – a fleet that was renowned for its smart livery and uniformed drivers.

Panhard 1910 This British built two cylinder cab was the 'other half' of the extensive W. & G. du Cross Cab Co. This cab was the first to carry a 'For Hire' sign on the roof. The support pole is just visible in the photograph. Note the unusual spotlight mounted in the centre of the dashboard and the weather shields following the banning of windscreens.

economical to run but depreciation was heavy. The four cylinder cabs had higher fuel costs but, being more sturdily built, depreciation was better. As the drivers paid for the fuel but gained nothing from the saving in depreciation, they were inclined to take out the two cylinder cabs. After 1911 when they were awarded the Extras they preferred the bigger cabs, because they could earn more Extras. However, the cost of fuel for the large cab was a bone of contention and led to a strike in 1911 for cheaper petrol than the 9*d*. per gallon they were paying. A Government Court of Arbitration subsequently fixed the rate at 8*d*. per gallon. However, the bigger vehicles put the proprietors into a higher taxation rate, which meant an extra £2 2*s*. per annum, thereby increasing the proprietors' costs by some £22,000.

The total loss of Extras, high taxation, and the penny a gallon on petrol they had to pay as a result of the Court of Arbitration award, was by current (1970s) prices approximately £1 million. In April 1911 a Government Committee of Enquiry set up by Sir Winston Churchill, then Home Secretary, recommended that the application for a fare increase by the proprietors of 1*s*. a mile should not be awarded. That decision virtually meant the end of

Argyll 1910 A later and more compact single landaulette four cylinder, 15 h.p. Argyll with many pre World War I features like artillery wheels, spare 'stepney', oil lamps, roof rack, and high bodied coachwork.

the big fleets and since then there has been a steady swing towards a greater proportion of owner drivers and small fleet operators.

The decision was unjust. The 8*d*. fare was laid down, whether rightly or wrongly, on the basis that the Extras belonged to the proprietors and the men paid for the fuel. The proprietors needed that fare increase; furthermore, it is quite likely that had the fare increase been awarded in 1911, London cab fares would now be 25 per cent higher than they are, at which figure they would be closer to the rates charged by their unlicensed rivals.

As a contrast to the position in London, the fare in Glasgow in 1909 was 1*s*. for the first mile and 3*d*. per quarter of a mile. Double fare was chargeable between midnight and 6 a.m., and on Sunday it was fare and a half. The first 56 lb of luggage was carried free, but over 56 lb and up to 112 lb a charge of 6*d*. was made.

The finale was yet to come. On 1 January

Unic (Gate) 1912
This 1912 Unic incorporated the gate change four speed gearbox with hand and foot control. The engine was a four cylinder cast en bloc. Other than this it was similar to its predecessors. Many of these popular cabs kept running until the mid 20s.

1913, the proprietors increased the cost of fuel to the cab drivers from 8*d*. a gallon to 1*s*. 1*d*. Immediately the men struck, refusing to pay the increase. Their slogan 'Why should labour be forced to pay for the action of capital' had a justifiable ring about it and was taken up by *The Times*, remarkably, this time, on the side of the driver. The strike lasted for three months, and achieved nothing. As a result of the strike the Fiat, De Dion-Bouton and the Universal Cab Co. never reopened their garages; not long after the National Motor Cab Co. Ltd and the Waterloo Cab Co. Ltd also had to close down.

At the outbreak of World War I thousands of cab drivers joined the armed forces; many were subsequently killed. As with World War II, petrol rationing caused problems for those drivers remaining in Britain and they were reluctant to undertake the longer journeys. This caused tension between them and the public as the drivers tended to pick and choose their fares. Many more fleets went out of service during the war. One of them the British Motor Cab Co. turned its entire garage over to war production, selling off its cabs to mushes. For those cabmen in the forces industrial strife had ceased, but for those still driving in London, the arguments and strikes continued. In 1917 after a six week strike the drivers won the right to free petrol, and a further strike that year brought the right of free entry to railway stations.

The proprietors were still further penalised by the Home Secretary's refusal to increase fares, even though it had been intimated that the Home Secretary would permit these if the proprietors agreed to the men's demands for free petrol. The fare was not in fact increased until 1920 when it became 1*s*. for the initial hiring for 1 mile and 3*d*. per quarter of a mile, plus 6*s*. per hour waiting time. By then the damage had been done and many proprietors had been forced to close down. Also, the price of the first cab to be built after the war, a Beardmore Mk I, in 1919, was double that of a similar pre-war vehicle. Thus the fare increase requested in 1911 was already out of date when it was finally granted in 1920.

LD·5768

Between the wars

These were lean years for the manufacturers, proprietors, owner drivers and journeymen. The immediate post-war period was chaotic, with far more drivers than there were cabs, whose numbers were some 3,000 down on the 1914 figure. In April 1919, Superintendent Bassom of the Public Carriage Office stated that approval had been given for a new cab and it was expected that some 200 would be produced each week, but they were not all destined for London.

The Licensed Vehicle Workers Union (L.V.W.U.) said that the shortage was partly artificial, because one large garage was holding back about 600 pre-war cabs. Another garage in Tooting held some 200 pre-war Darracqs and Vinots and were selling two a week – the Darracqs for £300 passed at the Public Carriage Office, and the Vinots for £200 unpassed. Though these cabs were nine to ten years old, the second hand asking price was, in the case of the Darracqs, nearly as much as when new.

In April 1919 the British Motor Cab Co. decided to discontinue running cabs and announced they were selling two cylinder Renaults, overhauled and ready for work, at £200 on the Hire Purchase or £180 cash. They also had 450 old type cabs that they were saving for demobbed drivers for £120 each; these were in running order, repainted, fitted with a taximeter, but not passed at the Public Carriage Office. The company had also sold off many cabs to dealers for conversion to light delivery vans.

In May 1919, Alfred 'Titch' Smith, President of the L.V.W.U., complained to Scotland Yard that more than 1,000 discharged soldiers, with licences, could not get employment. Cabs were standing idle because of the 10 inch clearance required by the new regulations. However Scotland Yard stated:

> The Licensing Authority has not insisted on the 10 inch clearance. The British Motor Cab Co. asked that this be waived in order that they could put 100 cabs on the road. Permission was given but the cabs were not forthcoming. In March, the Ford Motor Co. sought permission to place 500 cabs in London, though they were not up to standard. Again, permission was given because of the cab shortage in London. Nothing further has been heard from this company.

Against this controversial background William Beardmore Motor Co. then launched its Beardmore Mk I, the cab referred to by Superintendent Bassom. William Beardmore & Co., which was an extremely large engineering concern, made its cabs at the old Arroll-Johnston car company's works at Paisley, and the lesser known Beardmore car at its Anniesland works. Later, the taxis were to be produced at Anniesland, after car production had ceased.

Beardmore Mk I 1919 This was the first new cab to be produced after World War I. Built by Beardmore Motors Ltd of Paisley, Scotland, it heralded a long association with the cab trade. It was powered by a four cylinder, 16 h.p. engine with a detachable cylinder head and five bearing crankshaft, leather cone clutch and four speed gearbox.

A subsidiary company, the Taxicab & Motor Co., was set up with a capital of £250,000 to supply the Beardmore cabs, for cash or H.P. By November 1919 agreements had been completed and deposits had been paid on 1,120 cabs. Apart from the manufacture of taxis and cars, the parent company continued with its other activities. In 1928 the largest British aeroplane built prior to World War II was the Beardmore's 'Inflexible', a three engine monoplane commissioned by the Air Ministry and designed by Dr Adolf Rohrbach. The company had already been successful with the Beardmore Wee Bee monoplane in the first light plane competition to be held in Great Britain, on 4 October 1924.

G. H. Allsworth, the man who had given King Edward VII his first ride in a motor car, was managing director of Beardmore Motors Ltd, formed early in 1919 to manufacture taxis. Another founder was Lord Invernairn, then Sir William Beardmore. The first Beardmore taxi, the Mk I, was very successful and is still looked upon as the 'grand old man' of the cab trade. It was the first London cab built to suit the requirements of the trade as it had been designed in consultation with them. (Beardmores continued to do this before designing any of their cabs.) The Mk I had a dropped chassis, facilitating passenger access, a 16 h.p. engine with a five bearing crankshaft, and a four speed gearbox. The standard version cost £650 and a De Luxe model with interior lighting and starter motor cost £690.

Within three years, the Beardmore cab was followed by the Belsize, Fiat and Unic. Production of the Unic had already restarted in France. British imports were still very restricted, and it was only as a result of questions asked in the House of Commons that the Board of Trade gave a special licence to import these cabs in 1920. They proved very popular, especially as they had an excellent back-up service.

By 1925, several other makes of cabs had appeared. Most, like Mepward and F.I.A.T., were virtually non starters as they did not have time to get established before the Depression. The exception was the Hayes, described by mushes as a 'really beautiful cab'. It was Canadian with an American Continental engine, and it sold for around £200 cheaper than the Beardmore – one reason why it was popular with mushes. In 1926 a group of 109 mushes tried to form a 'Hayes' Club, but nothing came of it.

Beardmore Mk II (Super) 1924 Almost identical to the Mk I, the 'Super' standardised the successful features of the Mk I. This picture is of a rare three-quarter landaulette. Note the distinctive chassis frame similar in style to the 1908 Wolseley.

From 1924 onwards a new colloquialism was used in cabbing circles: drivers of the yellow cab were called 'Butterboys'. This cab was introduced by the famous Chicago firm of the same name who trained the drivers for the 'knowledge'. The term 'Butterboy' has been applied to newly licensed drivers ever since.

These cabs were operated by the W. & G. Co., formerly the W. & G. du Cross Co. of Acton, a firm that was also still running pre-war Napiers and Panhards. The cabs were assembled in Acton by the Turpin Engineering Co., a subsidiary of the Sunbeam-Talbot-Darracq Group. The latter Group had been formed to put a new Darracq cab into service, but the cab never materialised. By 1925 the connection with this Group seems to have been severed. In May 1925 an advertisement in *Steering Wheel*, the journal of the British taxi industry, refers to vacancies for drivers of W. & G. Yellow cabs, Napier and Panhard cabs, and repairs to any motor cab. Applications were invited to the Turpin Engineering Co. Ltd of Acton.

Until the Citroen cab appeared in 1923, no other cab had supplied electric lights as standard fitting, as many proprietors had preferred to rely upon oil lamps. Electric light kits for installation were supplied by several firms, notably C. A. Vandervell Ltd of Acton, and the British Lighting and Ignition Co. of Westminster. C.A.V. offered a lighting set from £18 18*s*. and some 200 of these were supplied to the Mount Pleasant Motor Cab Co. For £15 15*s*., free delivery B.L.I.C. offered a complete set consisting of a 6 volt dynamo, battery, cut out, a circular switch board fitted with an ammeter, two 6 inch double purpose side lamps, a taximeter lamp and tail lamp with the necessary belts and wires, with the switchboard arranged to give dim and bright lights.

The 1923 Citroens, which were largely owned by the London General Cab Co., cost

£540 – considerably less than the Beardmore. In 1926 the Citroens were reduced to £495 – a new Unic, at that time, was £625. If the Citroen was purchased on H.P. it required a deposit of £75 and instalments were £12 10s. a month. This, however, included a complete lighting set plus a year's insurance premium and taximeter rental.

Following the relaxation of the 'Conditions of Fitness', it was the chassis from this Citroen that in 1929 was used by the London General Cab Co. to carry their own 'Coup de Ville' bodies. This cab known as the 'General' was used mainly by the company, following their expansion after acquisition of the Red Motor Cab Co.

The Super Beardmore of 1924, which cost £625 without Extras, became a front runner because it was a good cab, and over an extended period its running costs fully justified its purchase. Until the 1950s Beardmores used the advertising slogan, 'For comfort and speed it's all that you need'.

The restrictive Public Carriage Office regulations in force prior to 1928 were largely responsible for many motor manufacturers withdrawing from the London cab scene. The 10 inch clearance rule simply did not allow design similar to that developing on private cars. The limitations on overall length and the 25 feet turning circle also presented difficulties. The efforts of firms like Beardmore, Austin and Morris, who concentrated on London cabs, eventually paid off. As a result the modern London cab has a pedigree unrivalled by any other purpose-built vehicle, with the possible exception of London Transport buses which, prior to 1933, came under the Public Carriage Office regulations.

After a Home Office Committee of Enquiry in 1927, the 'Conditions of Fitness' were changed to allow the 10 inch clearance to be reduced to 7 inches, and for advertisements to be placed inside the passenger compartment. The Committee of Enquiry had also recommended the abolition of the 25 feet turning circle and proposed that it should be 40 feet, but the Home Secretary overruled this suggestion. However the needs of the driver were still badly neglected, with no provision for a full screen or side screen, although brakes on all four wheels were allowed for the first time.

It was this last feature that made the Beardmore and Austin cabs (see chapter on Austin) superior to the first Morris-Commercial that had only rear brakes. The first Morris retailed at £395 including an English steel panel body, triplex glass, winding windows and shock absorbers. It was distributed in London and Liverpool by W. Watson Co. (Liverpool) Ltd, and was the result of a long association between William Watson and William Morris.

Beardmore's Mk III 'Hyper' followed in May 1929. The name 'Hyper', meaning

Beardmore Mk III (Hyper) 1929 This 'Hyper' model had an engine of smaller bore than previous models with a revised R.A.C. horsepower rating of 12.8, and it was 6 inches lower. This was London's first cab to have four wheel brakes. The body was further streamlined in 1930.

Beardmore Mk IV (Paramount) 1933
This 'Paramount' Beardmore was produced at a new factory in Colindale, and was a cheaper vehicle with a Commer four cylinder, 13.9 h.p. engine. Other than the rare saloon body pictured, it was available as single landaulette, three-quarter landaulette and six windowed saloon.

Below **Beardmore Mk V (Paramount Ace) 1936**
Incorporating many modifications of the 30s, the main difference was the wheel base at 9 feet 6 inches, which was 6 inches longer than previous models. Note the open side on the driver's left. Other than the single landaulette featured here, a three-quarter landaulette, saloon and fixed head saloon were available.

beyond or in advance of, was the result of a competition organised by Beardmores among existing owners of the Mk I and Super models. A study of the complete specification of this cab reveals how fuel economy was achieved, vitally necessary in cab operations. The newly patented Duplex manifold meant that each cylinder received the correct amount of fuel and air. The induction pipe was divided right down to the carburettor, so that on induction the cylinders could not rob one another of mixture. Previously this had caused loss of power and uneven petrol distribution, which was not only wasteful, but caused a rapid build up of carbon deposit requiring constant attention.

The trade had expected something good from the Beardmore stable and they were not disappointed. Many proprietors believed that it was the best cab so far produced, and they described it as elegant, with roomy interior, low centre of gravity, four wheel brakes and lower priced. The 'Hyper' weighed 25 cwt, and it was claimed that it would do 26 m.p.g. The horsepower rating was reduced to 12.8, which meant that the road tax was £3 per annum less than with the first Morris. The brakes on the Beardmore Mk III were for the

Unic 1920 This Unic cab, sold by Mann & Overton Ltd, was the same cab as the 1912 'Gate' version, except for re-styled bonnet and radiator. The illustration shows a driver attempting to pass his Public Carriage Office driving test.

Left **Fiat I.T. 1920** The Fiat shown here, known as the I.T. model, was built with a four cylinder, I,846 c.c. engine and was capable of 37 m.p.h. Few were licensed in London, but they were popular in many European cities. Note the disc wheels, a distinguishing feature of cabs in the early 20s.

Far right **London General Citroen 1929** Using the standard 1923 chassis, the London General Cab Co. at its extensive premises at Brixton manufactured these 'coup de ville' bodies covered with fabric. The cab's interior featured good upholstery, safety glass and an electric dictaphone for driver communication.

Below left **Citroen 1923** This was Britain's first Citroen cab with a four cylinder, 11.4 h.p. engine. The landaulette bodies were English built. Although they were never very popular, the London General Cab Co. did buy a considerable number.

first time fully compensated between front and rear and were of the internal expanding type.

In 1929, W. Gowan from Capetown designed and produced the 'Cape' body cab, with sliding doors, for Morris-Commercial. This was a two seater, but it was never licensed. However, a four seater version was licensed in 1930 and over 100 were built. An advertisement in *Steering Wheel* that year described this cab as 'unconventional, in that its doors still open and shut without any risk of either hitting a lamp-post or striking a pedestrian'.

Another novelty was the 'Chinese Austin', produced by the 'London General' in 1930. Complete hybrids, they comprised bodies from the firm's old Citroens, mounted on Austin chassis, and drivers were quick to give them their nickname. Another cab that did not succeed was the Unic K.F.1. which had a French built engine that had proved unreliable. After production had ceased in

London General Citroen 1929 This picture highlights the transformation of these Citroen cabs. The conversion was done to keep pace with the new style cabs following the relaxation in the 'Standards of Fitness'. Although licensed by the London General Cab Co. for their own fleet, many were sold to mushes.

France, it was built in Britain by United Motors Ltd under licence from Unic Automobiles Ltd. It was a long ungainly looking cab, reminiscent of the type of car used by American gangsters of the same period.

By 1931, the first Morris 'G' International had given way to the smaller version, marketed as the 'G2', but known as the 'Junior'. This was followed in 1934 by the Morris 'G2S' (Six), which was London's first six cylinder cab, powered by a 15 h.p. engine. This cab was said to have been built 'like a tank' and represented good value at only £385. It rapidly became a favourite with the drivers for road holding, steering and comfort of the passengers, with whom it was also popular. It came complete with direction indicators and a clear view screenwiper. The final pre-war Morris-Commercial cab, the 'G2SW', was similar to the Six; except that the modified engine with overhead valves was now rated at 14 h.p. It fully justified its nickname the 'Super Six'; it was more streamlined than the previous model, the driver's door had a drop window, and a speedometer was fitted.

Early in 1932 the London distributors of the Morris-Commercial cabs, William Watson & Co. Ltd, had opened their brand new premises in Grosvenor Road, by the side of the Thames. Considering the air of depression, it was a bold move; built entirely to their own plans, the new building covered 21,000 square feet. There was accommodation for 100 cabs, and the administration office was built above, commanding a view of the river. Three petrol pumps were provided for the drivers and, although this garage has changed hands several times since 1932, it still provides the London cab trade with good service.

Meanwhile between 1920 and 1924 much had been made of the two seater side car 'taxis' that were used in Birmingham, Glasgow

Citroen-Austin 1932
This cab is made up of a 1923 Citroen body which, having been discarded by the London General Cab Co. in favour of its own bodies in 1929, was later taken out of store and mounted on the Austin 12 chassis, to create this hybrid.

Morris-Commercial G-type (International) 1929
This was the first cab to be launched after the relaxation of the 'Standards of Fitness' in 1927. It was an 'International' model by Morris-Commercial, a newcomer to the trade. The engine was a four cylinder, 15.9 h.p. Modifications in 1930 included full windscreen, headlights, bumpers and four wheel brakes as standard fittings.

and Nottingham. Once fares had increased in London in 1920, a constant pressure was maintained to lower them. One way this could be achieved, it was suggested, would be to licence a two seater cab in London. In April 1925 Sir Joynson-Hicks, Home Secretary, set up a Committee to study the question of two seater cabs in London, though a similar Committee in 1921 had rejected smaller vehicles on the grounds that they were unsafe.

For once the trade was completely united, vowing no two seater cab would be driven in London. Despite this affirmation, the Committee found in favour of the two seater cab and the Home Secretary made an Order to that effect in April 1926. He also overrode the Committee's recommendation not to initiate a two tier tariff, and the fare for 'Jixis' as the two seaters were nicknamed was fixed at 9*d*. a mile. However apart from one 'Jixi' which was licensed by the Public Carriage Office for test purposes, not one ever plyed for hire and the General Strike of that year finally put pay to the plans of the Hammersmith firm of White, Holmes & Co. Ltd who were planning to build them.

The two seater cab controversy cropped up yet again in June 1932, when the Raleigh Cycle Co. announced plans for a Raleigh three wheeled two seater taxi. The company claimed a petrol consumption of 50 m.p.g. and the cab weighed 6 cwt. The single cylinder, air cooled engine would develop 6 h.p., and it was to have coil ignition, a four plate fabric clutch, a Sturmey Archer three speed gearbox and a kick starter. The chassis was built up from

Morris-Commercial G-type (Cape) 1929
This interesting two seater body was the idea of Mr Gowan from Capetown, hence its nickname. Built on the standard G-type chassis, the idea was to alleviate the danger of opening doors. Unfortunately, the Public Carriage Office felt the biggest danger was crushed fingers and only one prototype was built.

strong channel section steel and the body was mounted on progressive action, quarter elliptic springs; the wheel base was 5 feet 6 inches. However this cab got no farther than the Public Carriage Office and everyone sighed with relief.

The long running Beardmore success was continued with the introduction of the Paramount series: the Mk IV 'Paramount' in 1933; the Mk V 'Paramount-Ace' in 1936; and the Mk VI 'Ace' in 1937. Production ceased at the Scottish factory, the company moved from Scotland to new premises at Hendon, and work recommenced with the Mk IV. The 'Paramount-Ace' introduced in 1936 showed signs of a modern style of design: flared front wings; modern looking front; dropped glass window on the driver's door; and a screen separating him from the luggage compartment. Some drivers unkindly called it the 'Greengrocer's barrow', because 'All the best things are in the front'. There was a choice of three models: single window coupe saloon, the three-quarter landaulette and the three-quarter fixed head saloon. All models retailed for £435. The Beardmore Mk VI 'Ace', the last of the pre-war series, incorporated synchromesh on all four gears.

Production ceased with the war in 1939, and the company was busily engaged on war work, making aero-engine parts and gun replacements. However, in order that the London cab trade should have a new vehicle after the war, Beardmores co-operated with the Nuffield Organisation in carrying out operational tests with a prototype 'Oxford'.

Morris-Commercial G-type (Cape) 1929
This illustration shows the 'Cape' bodied Morris in St James's Street, alongside contemporary cabs. This design revised as a four seater cab was later approved on a Morris G.2 chassis in 1935.

Morris-Commercial 'G.2.S.W.' (Supersix) 1937 The 1934 Morris 'Six' was London's first six cylinder taxi. This, the 'Super Six', was a more streamlined version with the luxury of a full length driver's door. The six cylinder, 14 h.p. engine had overhead valves and the gearbox was four speed with silent third.

K.F.I 1930 The K.F.I was built by United Motors of Cricklewood. They were in fact British built Unics. The one illustrated is a Jones bodied version with a spare wheel mounted at the rear.

K.F.I 1930 The four cylinder K.F.I was supplied with many different types of bodies. One of the finest was by the famous cab company and coach builder, Goode & Cooper. The spare wheel on their version was mounted alongside the driver. A full windscreen and headlamps were now standard fittings.

Cabs at war

In anticipation of World War II the London County Council had, as early as March 1939, laid plans to mobilise London's taxicabs. Consequently, when war did break, 2,452 cabs were requisitioned for war work. This was out of a total fleet of 6,699, which, incidentally, still included eight horse cabs (seven Growlers and one Hansom). The dramatic reduction of the London cab fleet by about 37 per cent left many drivers unable to find a cab to work. The situation was further aggravated by the introduction of petrol rationing and a corresponding decrease in takings of 30 per cent. The ration was increased in October 1939 from 2 to 3 gallons of petrol a day, irrespective of whether the cab was doubled or not, and the drivers were told to make better use of the 190 ranks that had telephones. The situation was relieved somewhat when the younger drivers were called up, and many older ex-service cabbies were recruited to drive ambulances because it was felt that with their 'Great War' experiences they would not lose their heads. Because of their knowledge of 'short cuts', they were often first at the scene after air raids.

Provincial taxis were only allowed 20 gallons a month. W. Seaton of the Nottingham Streamline Taxicab Owners Association was the leading figure in protests to Sir Geoffrey Lloyd, the Minister responsible, for the ration to be raised. As a result, early in 1940, the provincial cabs ration was increased to the same as London.

Taxicab owners whose vehicles had been requisitioned by the Auxilliary Fire Service found employment driving their own cabs towing trailer pumps. For this they received £1 17*s*. 6*d*. per week for the cab and £3 per week for their services as drivers.

There were many fatal accidents involving pedestrians and drivers during the blackout. Bilking increased as passengers disappeared into the darkness without paying their fare. The Police refused to allow meter flags to be illuminated, yet bus route indicator boards carried a light. In 1941 the *Evening News* carried a story on how a cabbie drove down The Mall in the blackout. 'Easy', said the driver, 'if I knock a cyclist down with my offside wing, I'm too far right; if I knock him down with my nearside wing, I'm too far left. It's easy really!'

Meanwhile, production of cabs had ceased, although two prototypes being developed at the outbreak of war were approved in 1940. One was the Wolseley which was developed in conjunction with Beardmore Motors Ltd. It was run throughout the war and covered 100,000 miles. The other, the Watson cab, was developed by William Watson & Co., but was abandoned and never taken further than one prototype.

Mann & Overton Ltd kept going by turning their garage and repair shops etc. over to war production, but keeping part of the premises

Above **Austin LL with trailer pump 1939** The bulk of the 2,452 cabs requisitioned for war work were intended to be used for towing this trailer pump unit.

Left **Austin LL with blackout markings 1939** This Strachan bodied 'Low Loader' is still in the livery of the London General Cab Co., but has had blackout markings painted on the wings and the headlights covered over.

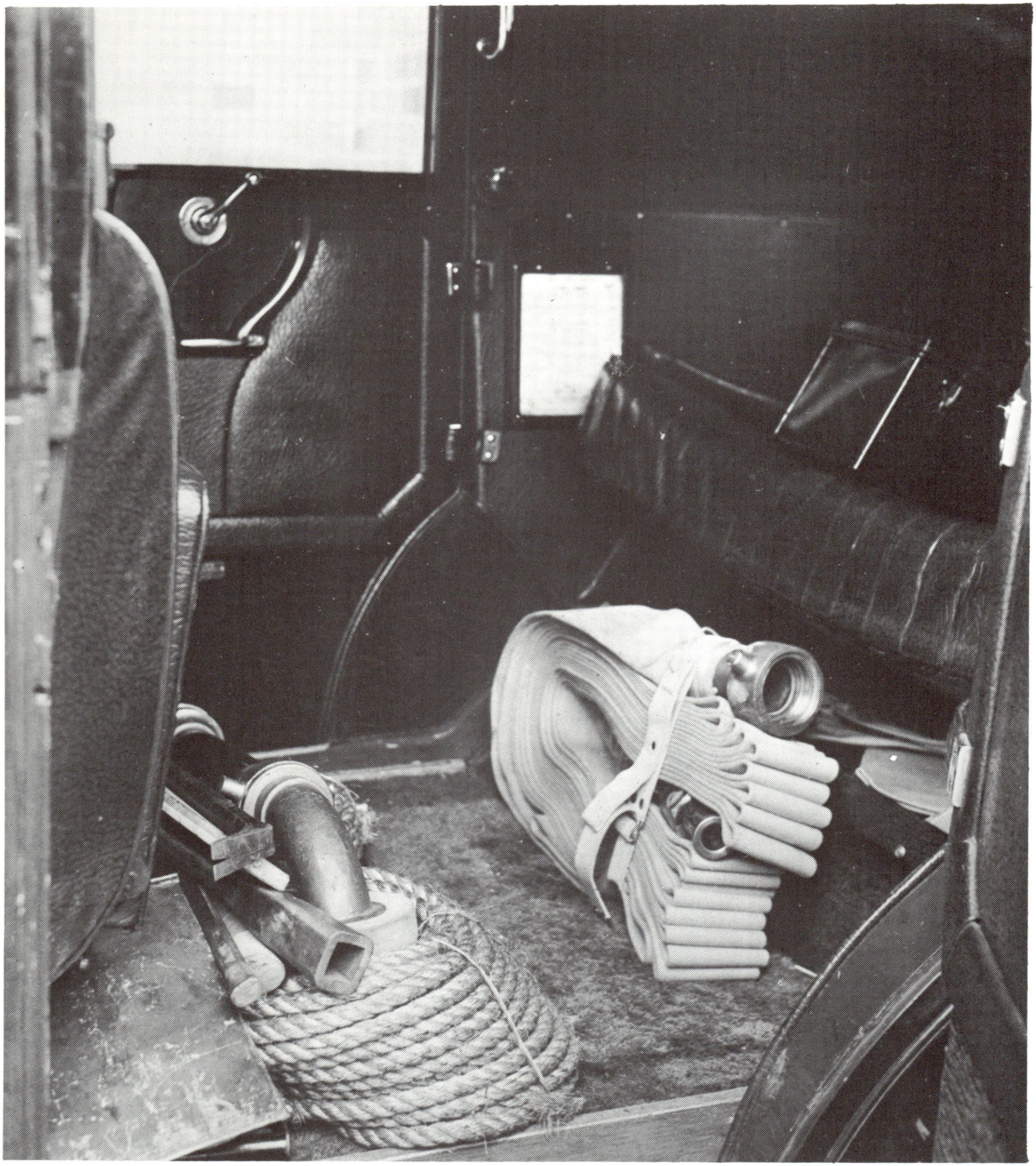

Left **Austin LL with fire fighting equipment 1939**
This interior view shows the extra work-load carried in addition to ladders and trailer pump in tow. Note the fare table still in position by the door pillar.

Right **Austin LL in A.F.S. livery 1940**
This photograph illustrates the ultimate livery of those cabs retained throughout the war for use in the Auxiliary Fire Service under the control of London County Council.

L.C.C.
LONDON FIRE BRIGADE
A.T. 131
AFS
DGO 183

as a depot for the repair and overhaul of cabs. With their main normal business activity, the supply of new cabs, at a standstill, they ticked over waiting for the end of the war.

Towards the end of 1943 there was a controversy in Parliament when John Mack M.P. asked that the number of taxis should be reduced in order to save fuel. The Home Secretary replied that cabs were already 37 per cent down and that there were not enough. The suggestion of another M.P. that journeys should be limited was given added strength by Police prosecutions of 92 drivers for refusing. Apparently there appeared to be no co-ordination by the Authorities on taxis and other forms of transport, commented the Press.

The Control of Fuel Order of March 1944 rectified this and limited a driver to a distance of 5 miles with any fare, unless a member of H.M. or Allied Forces, or Police Services acting on duty. It also applied to members of the forces returning from leave and several other groups including the Merchant Navy.

Of those cabs eventually released from war service less than half proved sufficiently fit to resume cab work. Even so, in 1945, 5,321 cabs were still licensed. The great majority were well over ten years old and many, despite shortage of labour and spares, soldiered on until the mid 50s.

Battle-scarred cabs 1940 This line-up features three battle weary 'Chinese' Austins. Of those cabs returned from war work, less than half proved fit enough to resume licensed cab work.

The Austin story

Austin Motor Co.'s association with the cab trade is often thought to have begun in 1930 with the introduction of the Austin Heavy Twelve/Four, distributed by Mann & Overton from their premises in Battersea Bridge Road, London S.W.11. However, as we have seen, it started back in 1906.

By February 1909, no doubt as a result of the change in the 'Conditions of Fitness' following the controversy surrounding the first Renault, Austins reintroduced their 1907 cab styled in a more conventional manner. The engine was brought forward, though the construction and design was unaltered. The body had a neat sliding sheet metal panel, fitted into the upper part of the window behind the driver's head – an improvement on the usual speaking tube on other cabs. These four seater cabs were run by the Urban Taxicab Co. of Avonmore Road, West Kensington, who had a fleet of ten. A slightly different version with a more utility styled body and a soft top sloping canopy over the driver was licensed in Edinburgh in 1910.

Later in 1910, the Taxi De Luxe Co., also of Avonmore Road, West Kensington, introduced nine Austin landaulettes. The four cylinder, 15 h.p. engine and chassis were of the standard Austin pattern, but the bodywork and upholstery were more luxurious. The livery was brown with the panels effectively decorated with black stripes. The mountings were brass, and the doors were fitted with coach style handles. The cab was also fitted with a hinged top half screen, and an anti-splash shield on the nearside kept the rain off the driver. Not to be outdone, Urban Taxicab Co. the following year brought out the latest type Austin taxi in which the cylinders were cast separately, the piston stroke had been lengthened, and the crankshaft had five bearings instead of three; the thermo-syphon cooling had given way to pump circulation. None of these early models appear to have survived World War I.

After the war the London cab trade suffered many blows. The most biting of all was in May 1927, when the Home Secretary reduced the fare from 1*s*. to 9*d*. a mile, as he had previously threatened to do if the trade rejected the two seater cab. In the resulting depression, sales plummeted for the Unic cab which had become very expensive. Consequently, Mann & Overton Ltd, who were then the London distributors of the Unic cab, turned their attention elsewhere, and in 1928 William Overton successfully negotiated with the Austin Motor Co. to purchase a quantity of Heavy Twelve/Four chassis. Mann & Overton's attention was drawn to this vehicle because of its success in Manchester and other provincial cities. They selected a number of high class coach builders to modify the bodies and other specifications to conform to London regulations. This combination of Austin motor chassis and Mann & Overton expertise

Austin 1908 This was Austin's first taxicab. A unique feature was the three cylinder 15 h.p. engine together with the clutch and gearbox being mounted on a subsidiary frame which was then suspended from the main frame in a central position under the driver. In addition to the roof rack, folding shelves each side of the driver also accommodated luggage.

Austin 1909 The Austins featured here are more conventional than their predecessor, although the basic design of engine and transmission gearing was the same. Put into service by Urban Taxicabs Ltd in green and white livery, this cab was the first to have a sliding partition for driver communication.

Austin 1910 This Austin landaulette had a four cylinder 15 h.p. engine and was a luxury version. It was put into service by Taxis de Luxe of Hammersmith, and was finished in brown with brass mountings; the panels were decorated with black stripes. Later versions had thermo-syphon cooling instead of pump circulation.

Austin (Twelve/Four) 1929 Based on the popular Austin 12 chassis, this four cylinder provincial taxicab was a success in Manchester and other provincial cities. Both landaulette and saloon bodies were built by the Elkington Carriage Co. Unfortunately, the turning circle, braking system and V-shaped windscreen did not conform to London specifications.

was to prove the dominating factor in the supply of taxis to London.

Within only one year this partnership gained a higher percentage of sales than the combined sales of any other makes on the market at that time. The table highlights this dramatic swing.

The first Heavy 12 appeared on the streets of London on 7 June 1930. It was owned by A. W. Barker who was, at one time, chairman of the London Cab Trade's Mocatra Athletic Club and was a greatly respected personality. It had a Dyer & Holton body, and the engine was of monoblock construction, 12.8 h.p. and side valve; lubrication was by gear pump, forcing oil to all crankshaft and camshaft bearings. The gearbox, which had four forward speeds and reverse, though not synchromesh, was classified by the Public Carriage Office for driving test purposes as central control, i.e. gear lever and hand brake were situated in the centre of the driving compartment at the driver's left hand. The brakes were actuated on all four wheels and the hand brake was applied directly to a drum behind the gearbox, i.e. a transmission brake. It was priced at £380 cash or £50 deposit and £11 monthly.

Since the introduction of the Beardmore 'Super' in 1924, nearly every cab until the Beardmore 'Ace' of 1939 was given a nickname. The Austin Heavy 12 was no exception. It stood almost 7 feet high and was 'head and shoulders' taller than any cab since 1919; inevitably it was named the 'High Lot'. In January 1933 the Heavy 12 chassis changed slightly because of a modification to the gearbox, giving synchromesh between third and top; thus it became the Austin 'TT' or 'Twin Top'. Apart from this there was little change

Deliveries of new cabs

Year	*Total*	*Austin*	*Beardmore, Morris etc.*
1928	266	–	266
1929	898	–	898
1930	706	271	535
1931	643	400	243
1932	513	309	204
1933	962	834	128
1934	1,413	1,111	302
1935	1,515	1,178	337
1936	1,182	875	307
1937	755	659	96

Austin 12 (High Lot) 1930 This Austin Heavy 12 taxicab, built to London specifications, was distributed by Mann & Overton Ltd. It was powered by the standard four cylinder engine, and the brakes were rod operated. The body on this cab was by the Chelsea Body Co. Driver communication was by telephone.

Austin 12 (Chinese) 1930 This strange hybrid, built by the London General Cab Co., consisted of discarded Citroen bodies mounted on Austin chassis. This is a three-quarter landaulette version. The nickname 'Chinese' was a derogatory term because the drivers felt 'puzzled' in deciding whether it was an Austin or a Citroen.

Austin 12 (Chinese) 1930 This front view of an Austin 12 chassis with the Citroen body shows distinctly the famous flat, chrome surrounded Austin radiator. The wheels are the standard 500 x 20 of the period. Note the bulb horn (still a requirement of the 'Standards of Fitness'), also the tool box on the running board.

Austin 12 (Chinese) 1930 A single landaulette version of the 'Chinese' cab. The majority of these Austin-Citroen hybrid cabs were sold to mushes. This particular one is being used for driving instruction by the Royal British Legion Knowledge School. Note the small round window at the rear, a feature of London General Cabs.

Austin 12 (Cape) 1931 This 'Cape' body was built by Strachans of Acton on the standard Austin 12 chassis. The cricket seats were on each side of the cab and inclined forward to avoid the sliding doors. The nickname for this style arose because the designer, Mr Gowan, originated from Capetown, South Africa.

Austin TT (Upright Grand) 1933
Basically the same cab as the Heavy 12. The distinguishing feature was the introduction of synchromesh on third and fourth gears, hence the 'TT' originating from 'Twin Top'. The nickname refers to the appearance, said by the drivers to represent an upright piano.

in the basic design of the Heavy 12, although the transmission brake was removed, the hand brake was operated to the rear wheels, and the front propshaft bearings were replaced with Hardy Spicer couplings. Though it was called 'Upright Grand', this name and the 'High Lot' were quite often applied to both the Heavy 12 and the TT. Between June 1930 and June 1934 some 2,200 of both types of cabs were produced.

In 1934 the basic design was changed by using a form axle instead of the crown wheel and pinion type; thus the position of the propeller shaft was affected. This meant that the floor could be considerably lowered and, in fact, nearly 7 inches was taken off the height. Inevitably, it was called the 'Low Loader' or the Austin LL. Otherwise, this cab was still very similar to the 'Twin Top' except for some minor alterations, for example to gussets, hand brake support brackets and coil ignition.

By then, Mann & Overton had captured 77 per cent of the London market and from this dominant position could afford to cater for the whims of fleet operators and mushes by offering an extensive choice of bodies. Without exception, these different body makers stamped their own individual flair on the cabs. Strachan's for example gave the Low Loader a distinctive rakish lean-back to the centre pillars; the roof luggage rack rails were quite straight and without ornamentation. The rear of the cab flicked out slightly at the base. London General's Strachan bodied cabs were painted and trimmed at their Brixton garage. The cabs also had only one interior light; no centre arm-rests were fitted to the rear seat.

Jones Brothers accentuated their roof racks with curled ends; the rear had a tucked in charabanc look, and the petrol filler recess

Austin TT (Upright Grand) 1933 This version of the 'Upright Grand' is a Jones three-quarter landaulette. Note the curtains, a popular feature during this era. Of the many high class coach builders who constructed cab bodies for Austin chassis, Jones Bros of Westbourne Grove were the most popular.

Austin LL (Low Loader) 1934
Following a rear axle improvement it was possible to build the Austin 12 cab 6 inches lower than previous models. Other modifications included the use of coil ignition instead of magneto. This is the standard Jones three-quarter landaulette. Note that this type of cab still retained the popular curtains.

though half moon in appearance was much deeper. The windows had tubular pillars, and their upholstery which was Dunlopillo cost £5 extra. On the Rickett's body, the rear protruded to form a squarish boot to hold the spare wheel; curly ends to the luggage rail and the rear mudguards flared out. The tool box was under the driver's seat, instead of on the luggage platform next to the driver, and the body generally was considered to be better quality than the average Low Loader body.

Several body builders persisted with the 'Cape' body design until 1937. On 14 August 1931 the Public Carriage Office had approved a 'Cape' body, fitted on a Heavy 12 chassis, and presented by Mann & Overton; per-

Austin LL (Low Loader) 1934 This 1936 version, with a rare body by Ricketts of Euston, has been restored and is still in running order. The easiest way to identify a Ricketts body was by the wooden window pillars and an enclosed recessed spare wheel.

Austin LL (Low Loader) 1934 This surviving 'Low Loader' has a Strachan body, with its distinctive lean-back on the centre pillars and an outward flare on the lower part of the body. The small round rear window identifies it as being an ex London General cab.

Austin LL (Low Loader) 1934 This cab was the standard Jones single landaulette. The Jones body could be identified by the roof rack with the accentuated end curl, the way the body at the rear tucked in, and the shape of the petrol filler recess.

mission was given for 12 vehicles to be licensed. There were also a few Strachan bodies, but little is known of when they were licensed. The first 'Cape' body to be fitted to an Austin LL chassis was presented by Mann & Overton on 8 November, 1934, and approval was granted on the 13th.

This particular 'Cape' body was built by the New Avon Body Co., of Warwick. The Public Carriage Office was concerned that the roof was not strong enough and that the driver's position was somewhat exposed. However, six cabs were licensed: BLE 985, BLW 894, BLU 177, BLU 178, BUL 941 and BUV 801. They were all introduced into service between December 1934 and February 1935. Approval was given for a modified version of the 'Cape' body on 5 May 1935, a driver's door was now fitted as was a sliding window for better communication between driver and passenger.

Two other versions of the Low Loader were also built: the 'Fishtail' and the 'Flash Lot'. The first 'Fishtail' was approved on 30 March 1935. Its body, which was by Vincent of Reading, was of a similar design and construction to many of the different types already in service, except for the almost oval shape door window frame and the rear panelling. This version was nicknamed 'Fishtail' as the rear panelling was distinctly tailed out in a curve, to provide access for a spare wheel which rested in a well; the boot

Austin LL (Low Loader) 1934 This picture shows a De Luxe body by Vincents of Reading, the only provincial coach builders used for 'Low Loader' bodies. Of interest are the hood-irons being enclosed inside, a feature also used by Goode & Cooper, a cab company that built their own bodies.

Austin LL (Fishtail) 1934 This interesting body was an optional extra. The main feature was the extended back panel to enclose the spare wheel. The cab shown is a Jones single landaulette.

Austin LL (Flash Lot) 1938 This streamlined cab was built on the Heavy 12 chassis with the same four cylinder engine. It was the last Austin cab with landaulette style coachwork. Note the full length driver's door. Production of this cab was limited, due to the outbreak of World War II.

lid was hinged at the bottom. The Index Number was BXK 112 and the chassis number 78245.

The last of the various bodies to be fitted on to Austin LL chassis was the 'Flash Lot'. The official description of the body was swaged, but it was probably the most streamlined cab to appear and gave a good indication of future design. This cab had constant balanced windows instead of winding windows, a feature of cabs ever since. The first 'Flash Lot' body was by Vincents of Reading, though Jones Bros and Goode & Cooper were to make them. The pattern design approved for this cab was originally submitted in July 1934, but 13 major defects were listed. Although Mann & Overton said they would present it again shortly, almost two years elapsed before they did so, on 23 June 1936. Many different types of Low Loaders worked through the war, and in some cases they were working in 1956 – nearly a quarter of a century's service.

Mann & Overton realised that even after World War II had ended, it would still be several years before a new cab could be in production. This could mean a gap of almost ten years between the production of the last Low Loader and the possible production of a new model. However some thought was given to this problem and gradually the shape of the FX3 grew on the drawing board. The production of the FX3 was a big project, and two prototypes, the FX1 and FX2, were built before the final version the FX3 was ready for approval. Mann & Overton had already decided that an all steel body was essential for quantity production and they had to find a large sum for tooling costs. Fortunately they

went to Carbodies of Coventry, because they had a good team, capable of building excellent products. The draughtsman was Jake Donaldson; the engineer, John Orr; and the Managing Director was the late Ernest Jones, who had a great 'feel' for cabs.

Details and pictures of the prototype FX2 were released in January 1946. The modern style was reflected in the completed chassis, and the front bonnet assembly, which had already been inspected by the Public Carriage Office. At this stage the bonnet was to open upwards (as with the subsequent FX4) but this was changed before the actual production stage was reached. Even so it was still two and a half years away from service as a cab. Approval for the chassis and the body was given on 24 October 1947, and for the rubber mat in the passenger compartment on 15 November of the same year. In May 1948 the final approval for the tinted rear windows was given.

The FX3 entered service in June 1948, almost 40 years after the first Austin cab had appeared in London. The driver was completely enclosed and an overlapping glass partition separated him from the luggage compartment, which was still without a fourth door. This extra door was fitted to the private hire car version in 1950. The FX3 engine was a completely new model, but had the same 16 h.p. engine that was used in the Austin 16 Saloon, produced after the war. It was lower than the pre-war LLs and the wheel base was nearly 2 inches shorter.

A novel feature was the fluid jacks to all wheels; they were operated from a hydraulic pump on the nearside of the engine and mounted on the bulkhead. The front and rear

Austin FX3 1949 This was Austin's post-war cab, and it was powered by a new four cylinder, 16 h.p. petrol overhead valve engine. Although still a three-door cab, the driver was now fully enclosed. The bodies were built by Carbodies Ltd of Coventry.

Austin FX3 American Version 1950 This Austin FX3 taxicab was licensed to work in New York. Although 4½ feet shorter and $750 cheaper than American counterparts, it was never a success, probably because New York taxi drivers would not accept a cab with manual gear change.

wheels could be jacked up independently or all four wheels together. The braking system was girling linkage, with two leading shoes on the front wheels. The wide flared front wings swept down to the apron on which was fitted a steel bumper. The price of £936 1*s*. 8*d*. included purchase tax; by 1952 this had risen to £816 plus £454 16*s*. 8*d*. purchase tax. This tax had been doubled in April of that year and despite attempts by some M.P.s acting on behalf of trade organisations, the Government showed no sign of relaxing it. Inevitably, the number of cabs began to decline, and by 1953 there were about 2,000 cabs less than in 1951. Even before the double tax, the number of cabs was dropping because of increasing costs, especially of fuel which was double the 1939 price. The FX3 petrol engine was not very economical, averaging 17 to 18 m.p.g. The double tax was a bitter blow. Even though the fares had been increased by 33 per cent in 1951 and the extra charge now covered all passengers over one, actual running costs had increased by more than 150 per cent not counting the rise in the cost of living.

Following pressure by the Transport and General Workers' Union and the London Motor Cab Proprietors' Association, the Government in the 1953 Budget went to the other extreme and abolished purchase tax on all taxis approved by the Metropolitan Police. The number of cabs immediately began to increase. This coupled with the advent of the diesel engine dramatically improved working conditions although the economies made by changing over to diesel were passed on to the passenger by retaining a low fare.

The first diesel engine to be used in London was a Borg-Warner; this was fitted to an FX3 by Dives Ltd of Stockwell. It was followed by the Standard Motor Co.'s 2 litre diesel unit, once used in the Ferguson Tractor, and was quickly shortened to 'Fergies' by the drivers. It was however terribly underpowered and it was not until Austins made their own 2.2 litre engine in 1954 that really satisfactory results were obtained. The FX3 remained in production, largely unaltered, until 1958; during its nine years of production 7,267 were made.

The current FX4 was introduced in September 1958. Again it was an Austin chassis with a body produced by Carbodies of Coventry. This cab had no running boards and therefore gave the impression of greater width, though in fact it was only 1 inch broader than the FX3. For the first time in a production model London taxi four doors were fitted and the driver's seat was adjustable up and down. By adopting independent front wheel suspension, it had been possible to move the engine forward, giving more space for the driver and passengers. The same Austin 2.2 litre engine was retained, but the cab was fitted with a Borg-Warner automatic transmission. It was also the first London taxi to have hydraulic brakes. Unfortunately, the design of the body did not allow for the built in jacking system which has been greatly missed.

The Austin FX4 has undergone many

Austin FX3 and FX4 1968 The two post-war Austin taxis working alongside each other during the overlap period. Many of the FX3s had their working life extended by provincial taxi work.

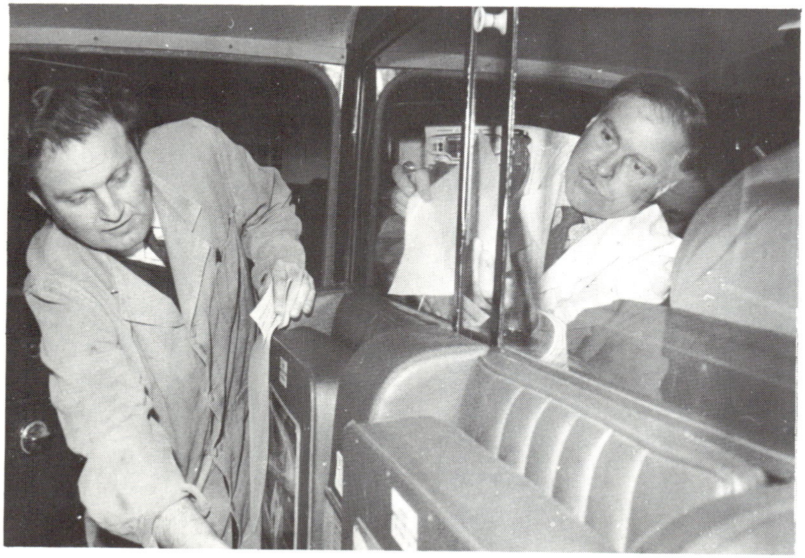

Above **Austin FX4 1958** The FX4 is now Austin's current production taxicab, and it was the first Austin cab to possess four doors as a standard fitting. It was powered by the 2.2 litre B.M.C. diesel engine and was the first cab available with automatic transmission as an extra. Note the circular disc used for driver communication.

Left **Austin FX4 1960** This interior view was typical of an FX4 until 1970. Driver communication was by a sliding vertical glass partition. The cricket seats clearly visible were well appointed. The picture shows Public Carriage Officers placing temporary fare increase tables inside prior to a meter change.

FX4 1970 Despite the introduction of the diesel engine, until 1974 FX4s were still available with the four cylinder petrol engine as an alternative. To compete with rising petrol costs, many of these petrol FX4s were converted to operate on propane gas by W. H. Cook & Sons Ltd, a famous London taxicab garage. Pictured here is the special gas tank in the boot, the spare wheel now being mounted in the luggage compartment.

improvements since 1958. The engine was replaced in 1972 with one of 2.52 litres; this extra power gave it something approaching the performance of a saloon car. There have been changes in design, notably to the bonnet and rear light assembly unit. Anti-theft devices are now standard fitting, so are quarter lights, locks to all four doors and a modern dashboard, with passing light and horn control adjacent to the steering column. The current (May 1976) price is £3,322.08 for the Automatic and £3,155.76 for the Diesel synchromesh. There is no car tax on the Metropolitan type FX4 taxi, whether or not it is used in London.

By any standards nearly 70 years of cab production, from the first Austin of 1908 to the present day, is a wonderful achievement. The original company became part of the British Motor Corporation in 1952 and was subsequently (1968) amalgamated into British Leyland. The association of Mann & Overton Ltd almost from the very beginning of the motor cab era was very important, as was their investment of huge sums of money in the FX3 and FX4 projects, thus ensuring that London had a purpose-built cab. The FX4 has its critics, but they are generally uninformed. A survey carried out by *Steering Wheel* early in 1976 revealed that 88 per cent of all drivers preferred the FX4 to any other type of taxi. They will not take lightly to any change.

FX4 1972 Body modifications in 1970 included the loss of the distinctive traffic indicator mounted on the roof in favour of a more conventional arrangement. Driver communication was by sliding horizontal glass partition and the cricket seats were of a more sparse construction. In 1972 the most significant modification was a powerful new 2.5 diesel engine. As seen here the FX4 was now available in a choice of colours.

FX4 1976 This unusual photograph shows FX4s decorated for the famous annual day outing to the coast for underprivileged children – an event organised by the trade. It also demonstrates the complete dominance of the Austin FX4 – being the only cab now in production.

To the present day

At the end of World War II, the Nuffield Organisation had a unique advantage over the Austin Motor Co. since their prototype had been running since 1940. They could therefore go into production with this cab by 1946 – almost 18 months before the Austin FX3.

On 21 June 1940 W. Watson Ltd had presented a cab at the Public Carriage Office, Index Number GGF 56 and classified as the 'Watson' landaulette. Approval was sought only for the one cab as production had been indefinitely postponed. The vehicle was not up to the standards generally required, but approval was given.

Less than a month later, on 15 July 1940, Mr Vaughan of Beardmores presented a cab made by the Wolseley Motor Co., Index Number EOM 844. This was the prototype run by Beardmores throughout the war, and which eventually became the 'Oxford' of 1946. W. Watson & Co. would have distributed this cab but some time previously Mr Watson had told the Wolseley Motor Co. that he would be retiring. The distribution of the 'Oxford' was therefore undertaken by Beardmore Motors Ltd.

With the introduction of the 'Oxford' the pre-war days of the folding hood were gone; mass production on an assembly line basis could not cope with the coachwork necessary for a drop down hood. However some ash wood was still used in the frame. The engine was overhead valve and had four cylinders giving 13.93 h.p. Its three bearing crankshaft was to cause problems later on as was the autovac fuel system. After its introduction in 1946, several refinements were made to the early 'Oxfords', including to the fuel system. The makers euphemistically described it as 'modelled on the limousine', although it still had a pre-war look. The total purchase price including purchase tax was £997 8*s*. 4*d*. A modified Mk II was introduced in 1949 and had larger brakes, heavy duty clutch and easy clean wheels.

The major differences in the Mk III were rear quarter windows, the centre partition window – which did not have a central pillar – and several other minor alterations. The same modified engine used in the Mk I was used in the Mk III but the earlier problems had been overcome. Production of the 'Oxford' series III, which was introduced in 1950, reverted to the Morris Motor Co.; Beardmores remained the distributors. Just under 2,000 'Oxfords' were produced between 1946 and 1954, compared with almost 5,000 FX3s over a similar period. The much lower figure for the 'Oxford' was due to its earlier introduction when business was lean immediately following the war, and the double purchase tax recession.

When the British Motor Corporation was set up in 1952 by the Austin and Nuffield merger, the 'Oxford' was doomed as by then the FX3 was the newer design and there was little point in producing two cabs from the

Post-war prototype 1945 This Jones prototype body was built on an Austin LL chassis to the specifications of the London Taxi Fleet Operators Federation, as being the type of post-war cab they would like to operate. Unfortunately, the Public Carriage Office rejected the vehicle because the passenger door height did not conform to the 'Standards of Fitness'.

Wolseley (Oxford I) 1946 The 'Oxford' prototype had been approved in 1940; thus Wolseley were enabled to launch the first post-war production taxi. This fixed head limousine made of pressed steel marked the passing of the coach built landaulette. The cab was powered by a four cylinder, 14.9 h.p. engine. A partition between driver and luggage was added in 1947, and a modified Series II was introduced in 1949.

Morris (Oxford III) 1950 The 'Oxford' was still produced by the Nuffield Organisation, but now under the wing of the Morris-Commercial Division. The Series III modification was mainly in body design; two rear quarter windows were added, and finally the artillery wheels were dropped. Following the Austin-Nuffield merger the British Motor Corporation stopped production in 1952.

Beardmore Mk VII 1954 This was Beardmore's first post-war design, and it incorporated gear change and hydraulic brakes. Initially a 1,508 c.c. Ford Consul engine was used, but in 1958 a Perkins diesel engine was made available. Windovers of Hendon built these cabs which were the last three-door cabs in production. A fourth door was introduced in 1965.

same stable. In January 1954 Beardmores announced that the 'Oxford' series had been discontinued but that there were sufficient spares at Hendon to last for ten years. They also intimated that a new Beardmore, the Mk VII, was imminent and that it would have surprising features in design and performance.

The last of the Beardmore series, the Mk VII came into service in February 1955. It had been exhibited at the Motor Show of 1954, and was presented to the Public Carriage Office on 14 December 1954; final approval was granted on the 30th. During January, drivers were invited to give it a test drive and sales commenced the following month. The most startling change was the construction of the body, which was aluminium with fibre glass wings; the early models had had a fibre glass roof but so many problems were encountered by the paintwork cracking and peeling off that the fibre glass was replaced with metal. The chassis was virtually a Ford Consul, with the standard Consul square monoblock four cylinder; overhead valve engine and the gearbox was also from the Consul.

In 1958, Beardmores fitted the Perkins '99' diesel engine to keep up with Austins 2.2 litre diesel engine. Although initially it was extremely noisy, modifications and sound proofing effectively stopped this. The front springing, semi elliptic mounted on the axle

Winchester Mk I (D) 1963 This was the first London cab to have a one piece fibre glass body. Other innovations included an illuminated recess step for the passenger compartment, full curved windscreen and the unusual 'Taxi for Hire' sign. The diesel engine was a specially silenced Perkins 4/99.

Winchester Mk II 1964 This was a petrol engined version of the Mk I, and it incorporated a four cylinder Ford Cortina engine, with a four speed gearbox and dry plate clutch. It differed from the previous model in that it was now all black. Many of these cabs were later converted to run on propane gas.

beam, was controversial, and many prospective buyers especially mushes were put off after the test drive. The engine mounts often gave trouble with the earlier models though within a few years most of these faults had been rectified. This cab was never sold in any great quantity.

Beardmores were thinking of a new model, Mk VIII, but it never got beyond the drawing board stage; London had seen the last of the Beardmore taxi. The firm closed its works in Hendon in 1969 and repair and maintenance were undertaken at the Clifton Garage, Maida Vale. In 1970 this garage also closed, and 51 years of association with the London cab trade had ended.

The only real break from traditional style came with the 'Birch' taxi, made by Birch Brothers of Kentish Town – a firm greatly respected by the trade. The cab was patterned on estate car lines: one passenger seated next to the driver but facing the rear, and three passengers seated on the back seat, which having been brought forward from over the rear axle gave more room. The luggage space was at the rear, and the luggage door opened from the pavement. These arrangements gave the driver considerably more room in which to keep his personal belongings. This one model was intended to work for six months in order to evaluate its possibilities, but in fact it continued to work for about four years and always evoked considerable interest among drivers wherever they encountered it. No others were ever produced.

Another experimental cab was the Metro Cammell by the Birmingham-based engineering group that specialised in railway rolling stock and buses. This 'Metro-cab' entered service with the London General Cab Co. in 1970, but the project was dropped within two years. Incorporated into this design was a collapsible steering column and servo assisted brakes – the first time that such equipment had been fitted as a standard feature.

Winchester Mk III 1968 Built on the same chassis as the Mk II, the Mk III body was completely re-designed, bringing it in line with contemporary styles. It was largely Ford equipped and was fitted with the Ford 260 1E engine – similar to that used in the Transit van.

Metropolitan-Cammell (Metro) 1970 Built by Metropolitan-Cammell-Weymann Ltd, the well-known builders of bus and coach bodies, this glass fibre cab was powered by a Perkins diesel engine, using a gearbox and transmission from the Ford Transit van. This prototype was licensed and operated by the London General Cab Co. for several years. Note the return of the running board.

Other vehicles to be introduced as London taxis were the Winchester diesel Mk I, the petrol version Mk II and the different body styling Mk III. The outstanding feature of the Winchester was the completely rustless one-piece fibre glass body. Also for the first time it incorporated an illuminated recessed step – a feature that had been sadly missed by many elder patrons with the FX4. The diesel engine was a four cylinder 1.62 Perkins 4/99 fitted with two silencer units. The Mk I which entered service in 1963 weighed only 27 cwt; fuel consumption was also very good.

The Mk II petrol version was almost identical except for the black body which replaced the two tone of the Mk I. It had a Cortina 1.5 litre engine with a five bearing crank and a four speed synchromesh gearbox. This cab came into service in September 1964. Both the Mk I, Mk II and the Mk III are now out of production. The Winchester was primarily designed as a mushes' cab in London and the provinces, and changes to the body design in 1968 gave it a much better look. The closure of Winchester Automobiles Ltd meant that the cab went out of production in 1972. Although a number of these Winchesters and a few Beardmores are still licensed, 98 per cent of London's cabs are Austin FX4s.

CONCLUSION

When Lucas Industries Ltd introduced their Lucas electric taxi in October 1975 they were probably ushering in an entirely new era of vehicles, as did the Bersey 78 years ago. Whether this prototype ever becomes the forerunner of a London cab is a matter for speculation. The Lucas taxi is designed to carry the same number of passengers as the FX4, although it is considerably shorter – a feature that the Commissioner of Police had noted in 1898 about the Bersey. A novel feature is the fixed driving seat with the control pedals which are adjustable to accommodate drivers of various sizes. The battery pack, again on similar lines to the Bersey, is carried in a detachable tray located under the vehicle floor. The lightweight lead acid batteries at present are only capable of giving an effective working range of 70-80 miles at a maximum speed of 55 m.p.h. Another problem is to find an alternative to the conventional battery charge facilities which could be quick and easy to operate and readily available in garages.

The cab trade is possibly on the brink of a considerable change. There is concern that a drop may occur in the standards that have been built up over the centuries, particularly the last 70 years. Undoubtedly, the London cab and the drivers are the envy of many capital cities, as frequently visitors to Britain testify. As no large city can survive without a taxi system, there is no reason to believe that this unique form of passenger transport with its specialised vehicles will not continue to adapt to its changing environment.

Lucas 1975 A full circle has been completed – the latest prototype cab is the Lucas electric taxi. The 50 b.h.p., 216 volt CAV motor which drives the taxi is capable of a 100 mile range at 55 m.p.h. This vehicle is over 3 feet shorter than the Austin FX4.

GLOSSARY OF TERMS AND NICKNAMES

Ace. Beardmore Mk VI cab.
Bilkers cab. Nickname for a type of horse-drawn cab.
Birdcage. Nickname for a Gamage-Bell cab.
Broom-off. To pass an unwanted job on to the next cab.
Butterboy. Newcomer to the trade.
Cape. Type of cab body with sliding doors.
C.G.V. Trade name of Charron cabs.
Chinese. Austin chassis with a Citroen body.
Clock. Taximeter.
Cock & Hen. Man and woman passenger.
Coffin cab. Nickname for the Cabriolet.
Covered cab. Early name for the Clarence.
Cricket seats. Rear facing occasional seats.
D.P. Dawfield, Phillips cab.
Double clock. A job over 6 miles.
Electromobile. Greenwood & Batley cab.
Fishtail. Austin 12 with a swept back rear panel.
Flash Lot. Austin 12 cab built between 1938 and 1940.
Flyer. Job to an Airport.
Full Flat. Cab rented for the week.
General cab. Modified London General Citroen cab.
Gladiator. 1910 version of the Vinot cab.
Gondola of London. Hansom cab.
Grand Old Master. Beardmore Mk I cab.
Growler. Clarence four wheeler horse cab.
High Lot. Early Austin 12 taxicab.
Humming Bird. Nickname for the Bersey electric cab.
Hyper. Beardmore Mk III cab.
Ickory. Rhyming slang for clock, i.e. Hickory Dickory Dock.
In and Out. A return journey.
Jewish Piano. Taximeter.
Jixi. Nickname for a two seater motor cab.
Junior. Morris-Commercial four cylinder cab.
K.F.I. British built Unic cab.
Knowledge. Learning the streets of London.
Legal. The exact fare.
Linkman. Doorman, at hotels, clubs, etc.
Low Loader. Austin 12 produced between 1934 and 1938.
Metro. Metropolitan-Cammell cab.
M. & O. Mann & Overton Ltd.
Mushes. Owner drivers.
Mustard Pot. Nickname for the early Argyll cabs.
On Point. First cab on a taxi rank.
Oxford. Post-war cab built by the Nuffield Corporation.
Paramount. Beardmore Mk IV cab.
Paramount Ace. Beardmore Mk V cab.
Pedals-to-Push. Nickname for the Adams cab.
Pieces. Luggage.
Punter. Passenger.
Roader. Job outside the Metropolitan Police District.
Senior. Morris-Commercial six cylinder cab.
Set. Accident, i.e. collision.
Shofuls. Jewish nickname for imitation Hansom cabs.
Stepney. Spare wheel, named after an early tyre company.
Sunstar. Nickname for the Star cab.
Super. Beardmore Mk II cab.
Super Six. Morris-Commercial six cylinder cab with overhead valves.
The General. London General Cab Co.
T.T. Austin 12 taxicab with synchromesh on third and fourth gears.
Tri-Bus. Three seater Hansom cab.
Upright Grand. Austin 12/4 TT cab.
W. & G. A cab belonging to the W. & G. du Cross Co.
Zeiger. Taximeter.

BIBLIOGRAPHY

Printed Primary Source
Acts, Public and General
Commissioner's Library, Scotland Yard
Parliamentary Papers, Reports and Returns and Evidence in Committee
Patent Specifications Indexes
Statutes of the Realm

Primary Sources M.S.S.
Records of the Public Carriage Office

Newspapers and Periodicals
Autocar
Cab Trade News
Commercial Motor
Daily Graphic
London Illustrated News
R.A.C. Journals
Royal Society of Arts Journal
Steering Wheel
Taxi World
The Times

Books
History of the London Taxicab, G.N. Georgano (1972)
Omnibus and Cab, H.C. Moore (1903)
Dictionary of National Biography

INDEX

Note: Numbers in bold type indicate an illustration.